insight text guide

Melanie Flower

Invictus

Dir. Clint Eastwood

First published in 2018, reprinted in 2019, 2025.

Insight Publications Pty Ltd
3/350 Charman Road
Cheltenham VIC 3192
Australia
Tel: +61 3 8571 4950
Email: books@insightpublications.com.au

www.insightpublications.com.au

A catalogue record for this book is available from the National Library of Australia

ISBNs:
9781925485929 (print)
9781925485936 (digital)

Cover design by Gisela Beer, based on a concept by The Modern Art Production Group

Printed by Markono Print Media Pte Ltd

contents

CHARACTER MAP

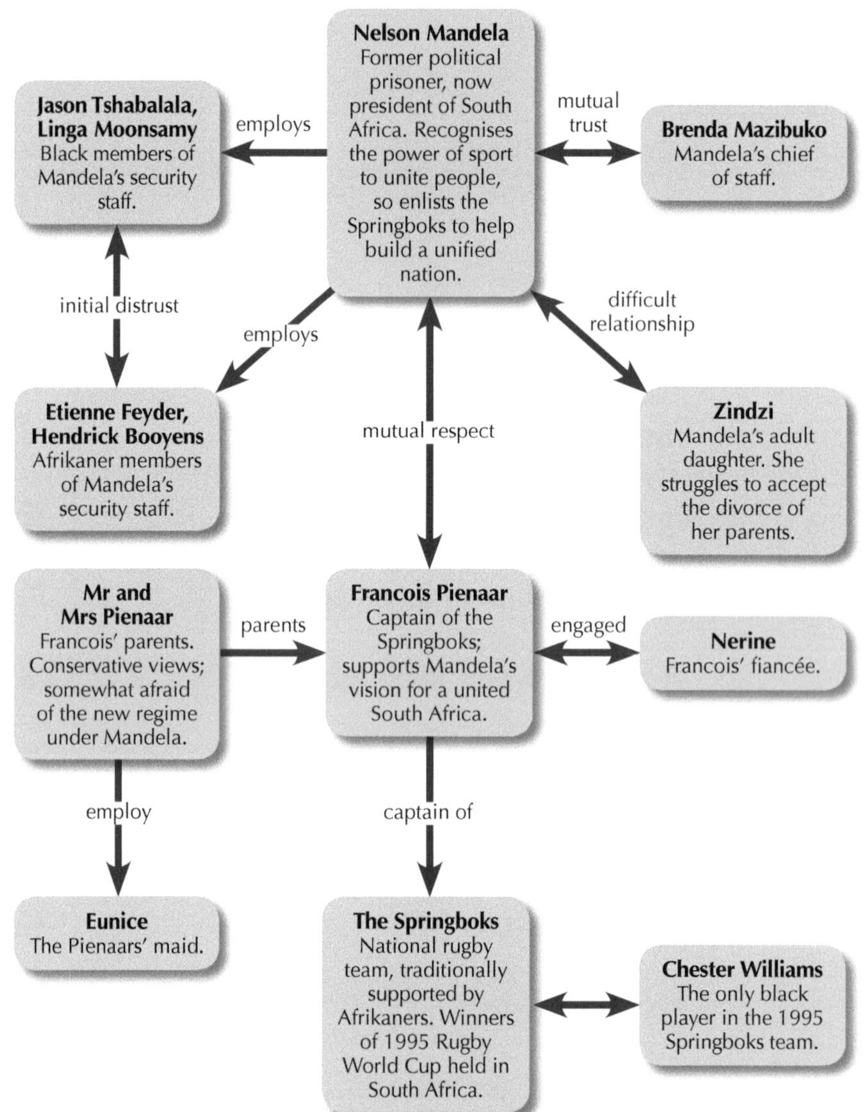

OVERVIEW

About the director

Clint Eastwood was born in San Francisco in 1930. He started his acting career in the television series *Rawhide*, a long-running western series in which he played cattle drover Rowdy Yates. From there he went on to make a series of 'spaghetti westerns' – westerns with Italian directors that were usually filmed in Italy or Spain. In the 1970s Eastwood moved into mainstream American films, playing tough policeman Harry Callahan in a series of four Dirty Harry films. He also played roles in some comedy and drama films.

In the late 1980s Eastwood made his directing debut with *Bird*. Since then he has directed more than thirty films, winning Best Director Oscars for *Unforgiven* (1992) and *Million Dollar Baby* (2004), both of which he also starred in. Other well-known films that he has directed include *The Bridges of Madison County* (1995), *Mystic River* (2003), *Letter from Iwo Jima* (2006), *Gran Torino* (2008), *Invictus* (2009) and *Jersey Boys* (2015). Eastwood has seven children and his son Scott Eastwood plays the role of Joel Stransky, a Springboks goal kicker, in *Invictus*.

Eastwood's films tend to be intensely character driven, and Mandela's statesmanship and integrity made him an irresistible subject for Eastwood.

Synopsis

Invictus tells the story of how Nelson Mandela harnessed the energy of the 1995 Rugby World Cup, which was hosted in South Africa, to promote unity within the country. The film opens with the release of Mandela from prison in 1990. A brief montage takes the audience through to 1994, when Mandela is elected president. His inauguration speech proclaims his determination to unite the people of South Africa, dismantle apartheid and address the disharmony this policy will create. His first days in government are marred by racial conflict and fear, and the task ahead of him seems impossible. Newspaper headlines on his first day in office question his ability to run a country – a question that Mandela acknowledges as legitimate.

Mandela's first challenges are to ease the fears of the largely white Afrikaner parliamentary-office staff, and unite his two distinct security teams; one black (his personal bodyguards) and the other Afrikaner (the presidential guards). The way he handles these challenges demonstrates his signature style, which is to empathise, connect, and address fear directly. He reassures the Afrikaner employees that he needs their help, and he explains to his security staff that they need to represent the rainbow nation, and must therefore be ethnically diverse. He asks his head of security, Jason Tshabalala, to put aside his fear and understand that this is where reconciliation and forgiveness must start.

While searching for a way to resolve the racial tensions within South Africa, Mandela attends a rugby game between England and the South African team, the Springboks. He notes that only the white spectators are supporting the Springboks. The black members of the crowd support England, in a show of defiance against a team which, to them, represents apartheid and colonial rule. Mandela realises that rugby could be a vehicle for reconciliation, particularly with the World Cup due to be played in South Africa in the following year.

When Mandela hears that the South African National Sports Council (NSC) is planning to abolish the Springbok colours, name and emblem, he appeals to the Council to reconsider. He understands that the Afrikaners (or Boers) love their green and gold, and if they lose their team they will lose an important part of their identity. His goal is to unite all South Africans behind the rugby team, something that will be impossible if the Afrikaners are alienated.

Mandela enlists the support of Francois Pienaar, the captain of the Springboks. Over afternoon tea the two men realise they have similar approaches to leadership; under Mandela's guidance, Pienaar works to unify his team and make it a cohesive force to be reckoned with. Mandela encounters opposition from members of his government and staff, who do not understand what they see as his obsession with a mere game. He explains that, without unity, the other, bigger problems cannot be resolved.

Pienaar is impressed by Mandela's vision, and shares his belief in the power of words and music to motivate others. He embraces Mandela's view of the team as representing a new, unified South Africa, and he encourages the Springboks to embrace this position. The players run rugby-coaching clinics in disadvantaged townships, and as they grow more united the team becomes more competitive in the looming World Cup competition. At the same time the Springboks begin to garner support from a broader section of the population, developing a fan base among the black South Africans.

By the time the World Cup competition begins, the Springboks are working well as a team and have great support from their country. Pienaar takes them to Robben Island, where Mandela was imprisoned for almost two decades. This excursion helps the players to understand Mandela's vision for the Springboks to become a symbol for a united South Africa, and inspires them to keep striving for the World Cup.

As Mandela travels the world seeking to rebuild international relationships, which suffered under apartheid, the Springboks progress through the rounds of the World Cup. They reach the final, and are matched against the New Zealand All Blacks – a dominant and undefeated team. This is the film's climax. The Springboks prove that, while their skills may be less impressive than the All Blacks', their fitness is extraordinary and they are able to outlast the New Zealand team. In a tight match which goes into extra time the Springboks narrowly defeat the All Blacks, fifteen points to twelve.

At the trophy presentation, Mandela and Pienaar each acknowledge what the other has done for their country. The people of South Africa are united in their celebration of the Springbok victory, and the film ends with jubilation and an overwhelming sense of national pride. Mandela sits back in his car as he journeys home, and enjoys the celebrations of the rainbow nation taking place all around him.

Character summaries

Nelson Mandela

Nelson Mandela is the central character of the film. After twenty-seven years incarcerated as a terrorist for his protests against the apartheid regime, he is released from the prison on Robben Island in 1990, and four years later is elected the first black president of South Africa. He takes an unexpected approach to this role, striving to create unity through forgiveness and reconciliation rather than seeking revenge for the injustices experienced under the previous Afrikaner governments. His statesmanship allows him to bring his people together, using the national rugby team, the Springboks, as a common unifying element.

Francois Pienaar

Pienaar is the white Afrikaner captain of the Springboks, the national South African rugby team. He is inspired by Mandela to lead his team to victory in the 1995 Rugby World Cup, despite the fact that the Springboks have only recently returned to international competition after years of being boycotted.

Jason Tshabalala and Linga Moonsamy

These men, along with three other black security guards, are determined to protect their leader, whom they have been working for since his days in the ANC (African National Congress). They refer to Mandela as Madiba, which is a Xhosa clan name used as a sign of respect. They are proud to work so closely with the man who is instrumental in addressing inequality in South Africa, and their loyalty to Mandela is unwavering even when they do not understand his decisions. They are initially distrustful of the Afrikaner security team sent to boost their numbers. They are frequently heard to express their dislike for rugby, which they see as being representative of the apartheid era.

Etienne Feyder and Hendrick Booyens

Etienne, Hendrick and two other Afrikaner men are appointed to Mandela's bodyguard after Jason requests additional staff. They are Special Branch policemen who have extensive experience protecting the previous president, de Klerk, and their military background means they are highly trained. However, they initially struggle to integrate with Mandela's existing black security team. They are passionate Springbok fans.

Brenda Mazibuko

Brenda is Mandela's chief of staff. She is a driven woman who seems to be always focused on work. Mandela appreciates her advice and support, although he does not feel bound by it. Brenda does not like rugby, and struggles to understand Mandela's commitment to the Springboks.

Mr and Mrs Pienaar

Francois' parents are middle-class South Africans. They are afraid of the changes they anticipate under Mandela, and are heavily influenced by the South African media.

Eunice

Eunice is the Pienaar family's maid. She is very proud of Francois, and of his connection to Mandela – a man she admires enormously.

Zindzi

Zindzi is one of the daughters of Nelson and Winifred (Winnie) Mandela; Nelson separated from Winnie in 1994 and they were divorced in 1996. Zindzi is resentful of the toll her father's political life has taken on her family, and she disagrees with Mandela's goal of reconciliation. The father-daughter relationship is strained as a result.

Sipho

Sipho is a teenage boy who represents the disenfranchised and disadvantaged black youth of South Africa. He appears in key scenes throughout the film, and his journey mirrors that of many poor South Africans as they move towards unity. His role in the film is a minor one, but he represents the majority of black South Africans.

BACKGROUND & CONTEXT

Clint Eastwood was inspired to make *Invictus* after reading John Carlin's 2008 book *Playing the Enemy: Nelson Mandela and the Game that Made a Nation*. Eastwood seized upon the story of the 1995 Rugby World Cup as a manageable way to explore Nelson Mandela's leadership and legacy. Mandela was imprisoned as a terrorist in 1963, released in 1990, won the Nobel Peace Prize in 1993 and was elected the first black president of South Africa in 1994. In 1995, when *Invictus* is set, he is ruling a country torn apart by years of apartheid (literally meaning 'separateness') and faces the difficult task of finding a way to unite South Africans and dismantle the racist social structures that have been in place for decades. Rather than trying to explore all aspects of Mandela's eventful life, Eastwood focuses on the way Mandela encourages reconciliation by developing the Springboks rugby team into a national symbol of unity for post-apartheid South Africa.

While the film is ostensibly about rugby, in fact it is more about Mandela's ability to harness the game of rugby as a way of uniting a nation. Eastwood's Mandela is a true statesman, charismatic and sensitive to the needs of his nation. His awareness of the power of sport, and his ability to use the media and language to begin rebuilding his country, are clearly shown through Eastwood's depiction of the South African president.

White colonisation and the Afrikaner people

Europeans first settled South Africa in 1652, when the Dutch East India Company (VOC) established a colony on the Cape of Good Hope. This was intended as an outpost for the VOC trading business, but developed into a thriving settlement made up of the Dutch, French Huguenots fleeing religious persecution in France, and German soldiers or sailors returning from service in Asia. These largely Dutch settlers initially cooperated with the indigenous population, but over time relations became more aggressive as black South Africans were forced from their land and many were enslaved. The white settlers were collectively known as Boers, which is Dutch/Afrikaans for farmer.

By 1806 Dutch power was decreasing, and the British Empire obtained control of South Africa. Within ten years thousands of British immigrants started arriving in the colony, known as Cape Colony. Many of the Boers moved further inland, establishing their own autonomous colonies in the Transvaal region in the north of the country. Over the next century the white population of South Africa continued to grow as a result of immigration, and by 1865 nearly 200 000 Europeans had made their home in South Africa. The first national census was held in 1911, and indicated a white population of 1.3 million people. At its peak in 1990 the white population of South Africa was around five million, making up just fourteen per cent of the total population. Many white South Africans have since emigrated, and today only nine per cent of the people are considered white.

History of segregation

South Africa has a long history of segregation, starting with European colonisation in the nineteenth century, before the official policy of apartheid was imposed.

In 1913 the Land Act was passed, which restricted black and coloured South Africans' access to land, forcing them to live in townships and restricting access to land. It was this Act that led to the creation of the resistance organisation that became the African National Congress (ANC), then known as the South African National Native Congress. In 1925 the SANNC adopted the Xhosa song 'N'kosi Sikelel' iAfrica' as its official anthem – which is why in *Invictus*, when Mandela introduces this as an additional South African national anthem, the (white) Springboks dismiss it as 'a terrorist song', with one of them noting that 'they used to arrest you for singing it' (Scene 14).

Tensions between black, white and coloured South Africans were further exacerbated by the Great Depression after World War I and the advent of World War II, as the economy suffered and the Afrikaner government scrambled to maintain its own power, at the expense of the majority of citizens.

Apartheid was first imposed in South Africa in 1948, when the entirely white Afrikaner National Party came to power. Its main goal was to separate South Africa's white minority from its non-white majority and, by diminishing the power of the opposition, ensure that the white minority retained government. The Afrikaner leaders aimed to decrease the political power of their opposition by dividing non-white South Africans on the basis of race and tribal affiliations. They introduced a raft of measures that privileged the Afrikaners and prohibited virtually all interactions between black Africans, coloured (other and mixed race) and white South Africans. Non-white South Africans were forced to live in separate areas from whites, and were not allowed access to any public facilities provided for the white citizens. They were also barred from participation in government. The government removed black (Bantu) and coloured people from their land, resettling them in overcrowded and impoverished townships. Prime real estate was reserved for the white population, and others were forced to seek authorisation and carry documentation (passbooks) if they needed to pass through restricted areas.

In protest the African National Congress moved to represent non-white South Africans. This organisation initially organised nonviolent demonstrations and protests, but these had minimal effect and by 1952 ANC actions became more overtly aggressive. A mass meeting in 1952 saw black and coloured South Africans burning their passbooks – an action which led to 150 people being charged with high treason. The situation continued to worsen and in 1960 Afrikaner police fired upon an unarmed group of protesters in Sharpeville. It was clear to non-white South Africans that the situation was unlikely to be resolved through peaceful protest, and so the military wing of the ANC (the Umkhonto we Sizwe – Spear of the Nation) was established under the leadership of Nelson Mandela.

The Afrikaner government responded aggressively to this new threat, and Mandela was arrested as a terrorist in 1963. His lengthy incarceration attracted international attention, and in 1973 the United Nations denounced apartheid. The UN stance was strengthened in 1976, when thousands of black children in Soweto, protesting against the imposition of Afrikaans as the language of instruction in schools, were fired upon with tear gas and live rounds. This drove the UN to impose an embargo on selling arms to South Africa. In 1985 the US and UK imposed trade sanctions on South Africa, as the world's criticism of the racist policy grew.

Of most direct relevance to *Invictus* is the UN's 1985 decision to adopt the International Convention against Apartheid in Sports, placing further pressure on South Africa to dismantle the system. This convention effectively eliminated South Africa from the international sporting arena, which is why the Springboks are referred to by de Villiers in the film as 'unprepared to re-enter the world of top-notch international rugby' (Scene 6). This extended exclusion from international competition makes the Springboks' eventual success even more extraordinary.

The South African government, led by Pieter (PW) Botha, implemented some reforms in response to the approbation of the rest of the world. Pass laws (the requirement for non-whites to carry identification papers, known as passbooks) were abolished, and the ban on inter-racial relationships was lifted. However, this was widely regarded as too little, too late, and Botha was forced to step aside for the more progressive government of FW de Klerk. It took almost ten years, but in 1994 de Klerk, working closely with Mandela after his release from prison, dismantled the final pieces of legislation that supported apartheid. Free, democratic elections were held later that year, and a coalition government with a non-white majority, led by Nelson Mandela, was appointed. Mandela and de Klerk shared the 1993 Nobel Peace Prize for their tireless efforts to bring about a peaceful end to the apartheid regime.

Mandela's inauguration speech, which is partially re-enacted as part of the opening montage of *Invictus*, states that 'never, never and never again shall it be that this beautiful land will again experience the oppression of one by another, and suffer the indignity of being the skunk of the world' (Scene 1). From the very start of his leadership Mandela makes it clear to South Africa and the world that he will not accept racism or apartheid, a position that harks back to the statement he made during his 1964 trial for treason:

> During my lifetime I have dedicated my life to this struggle of the African people. I have fought against white domination, and I have fought against black domination. I have cherished the ideal of a democratic and free society in which all persons will live together in harmony and with equal opportunities. It is an ideal which I hope to live for and to achieve. But if needs be, it is an ideal for which I am prepared to die. (Mandela 1964)

Faced with the difficult task of uniting a nation that, until recently, has been deeply divided, Mandela takes advantage of the 1995 Rugby World Cup as an opportunity to bring his people together in support of a common goal. He regards this event as a chance to present South Africa to 'a billion people, watching us … a great opportunity' (Scene 12). By showcasing the Springboks rugby team as a microcosm of a unified South Africa, Mandela is able to turn a sporting event into a moment of national pride that all South Africans, regardless of colour, can celebrate. He is also able to show the world that he is leading a new, more tolerant South Africa.

South Africa continues to face many challenges; while Eastwood's film focuses on the positive outcomes of the rugby tournament, it is fair to suggest that South Africa today is still a country divided by its past. However, Mandela's achievement with the 1995 Rugby World Cup is to give his people an opportunity to see what unity looks like. Having seen the positive possibilities, the citizens of this troubled nation are likely to be more open to strategies which can bring unity on a more permanent basis.

GENRE, STRUCTURE & LANGUAGE

Genre

The online film database IMDb categorises *Invictus* as 'Biography, Drama, History', which illustrates the challenge of classifying this film within a single genre. The film clearly includes important elements of history and biography, focusing on the facts of the lives of two main individuals – Nelson Mandela and Francois Pienaar, and considering how their lives fit into a particular moment in history. Simultaneously this creates a challenge for Eastwood, as he is put in the position of trying to create suspense and interest in a sporting event that has a widely known outcome. He does this in part by closely examining the experience of specific individuals.

The blending of genuine media footage with re-enactments, particularly during the opening montage, gives the film authenticity and adds weight to Eastwood's representation of events. This sense of authenticity is further enhanced at the end of the film (Scene 27) when historic photographs and film footage are shown during the credits. The effect of this is to emphasise to the audience that this biopic is based on a true story, even though at times it can feel a little contrived.

Despite the 'true story' nature of the film, Eastwood still succeeds in including elements that can see *Invictus* classified as a drama. While many viewers may be aware of South Africa's success in the 1995 Rugby World Cup, Eastwood manages to create suspense by strategically withholding information about how this feat was achieved. At the same time he introduces several subplots, which serve to enhance the tension and increase the drama. These subplots include the developing relationship between Mandela's black and Afrikaner security teams; the ongoing narrative of Sipho, who represents the impoverished black youth of South Africa; the familial relationships of Nelson Mandela and Francois Pienaar; and the role of the media in influencing South Africa's response to Mandela's leadership.

It is important to acknowledge that this film is a dramatic reconstruction of the events around the 1995 Rugby World Cup, not a documentary. While Eastwood and scriptwriter Anthony Peckham have remained largely true to the information included in John Carlin's biographical novel, the film must be regarded as a dramatisation of events.

Structure

Invictus consists of several linear narratives, all linked by the common thread of the Rugby World Cup. The primary narrative explores Mandela's efforts to unite South Africa behind the Springboks, and considers the relationship between Mandela and Pienaar as they work together to achieve this goal. This storyline is Eastwood's main focus. He carefully develops the relationship between Pienaar and Mandela, starting with the two men being in awe of each other, then examining how they become friends united by a common, ambitious goal. This mainly linear narrative provides a framework for the rest of the film, with flashbacks and other storylines occurring within or closely alongside this narrative, rather than separately.

In addition to the central focus, Eastwood includes several secondary narratives that are played out in parallel with the central storyline. This serves to demonstrate the breadth of experience of apartheid, giving a voice to people from a range of backgrounds. The character of Sipho appears at regular intervals throughout the film. He represents the impoverished and disadvantaged black and coloured people of South Africa, and his growing acceptance of the Springboks, as well as his increasing interactions with wider South African society, mirrors the journey undergone by many South Africans during this time. By the end of the film, Sipho is engaging comfortably with the Afrikaner policemen, illustrating his increasing confidence and acceptance. Mr Pienaar, Francois' father, undergoes a similar transformation. He progresses from having little interaction with Eunice, the Pienaars' black servant, to allowing her to attend the World Cup with his family.

Both of these subplots, microcosms of a nation that is slowly coming together, demonstrate the improving relationships between black and white South Africans.

One of the most important secondary plot-lines explores the changing relationship between Mandela's black security team and their new white Afrikaner colleagues. Eastwood uses this subplot to illustrate the journey of reconciliation and forgiveness occurring across South Africa. While Jason and his team are initially distrustful of the Afrikaner security team led by Etienne, Mandela insists that they learn to work together. A grudging respect develops, and by the time the Springboks reach the semifinals the two security teams are united enough to play a lighthearted game of rugby in Mandela's back garden (Scene 18).

In contrast to this, Mandela's daughter Zindzi represents the black South Africans who struggle with the notion of forgiveness. Zindzi's difficult relationship with her father, along with the complete absence of her mother from his life, illustrates Mandela's humanity and reveals the extent of the sacrifice he has made for his country. Zindzi resists reconciliation, telling Mandela that she doesn't like seeing him shake Pienaar's hand because Pienaar reminds her of 'the policemen' who forced her family 'out of our house' while Mandela was in jail (Scene 11). Despite her initial doubts, even Zindzi is shown to be caught up in the excitement of the World Cup final match, which suggests that even the most resistant South Africans can eventually be won over.

The intertwining of these multiple linear narratives allows Eastwood to explore the events of the 1995 World Cup campaign in South Africa from a number of perspectives. While his central focus remains on Mandela and Pienaar, by including other characters he provides an insight into the way various groups within South Africa respond to the events of that time.

Language

Vocabulary

Invictus uses spoken language very deliberately to enhance the narrative. While the dialogue is predominantly in English, many of the actors speak with South African accents. Some minor characters such as office staff and the charity worker who offers Sipho a Springboks jersey have English accents. This serves to remind audiences of the film's setting, and adds an air of authenticity to the film. The variety of accents highlights the differences between the South African citizens, illustrating the challenges facing Mandela.

Many scenes are introduced with brief snippets of dialogue in a language other than English. Rather than rely on subtitles Eastwood has his characters switch to English after establishing that a different language is being spoken. This technique can be seen when Mandela soothes his staff by addressing them in Afrikaans (Scene 3), as well as in his use of Xhosa when addressing the National Sports Council (Scene 7). In both scenes the initial dialogue is not spoken in English, demonstrating Mandela's multilingual skills. While he presents the potential of language as a unifying force, Eastwood also illustrates the divisive nature of different languages when he shows that Jason and Linga are unable to read the Afrikaans headline on a morning newspaper (Scene 2), and are unable to understand the Afrikaner security guards when they address each other in Afrikaans. Audiences feel the same brief confusion before the dialogue is translated, giving the viewer a small taste of the challenges faced by people who do not share a common language.

Cinematic language

As well as the dialogue, Eastwood uses cinematic language to convey meaning. This includes the use of verbal, visual and aural elements, as well as the deliberate use of filming and editing techniques. These elements function in a similar way to language use in a written text, providing context, emphasis and pace.

An example of this can be seen in an early moment in the film, when Mandela, Jason and Linga are out for their regular dawn walk (Scene 2). As the men stroll through the deserted streets, a van is shown driving erratically, speeding through stop signs. The accompanying sounds of squealing tires and ominous music add to the tension, and when the van is shown driving through an intersection the men have just walked through, the audience feels quite apprehensive. The tension is released when the van pulls up and the driver delivers a pile of newspapers, which feels a little anticlimactic. However, by creating this sense of danger Eastwood succeeds in not only engaging the audience, but also presenting the media – represented by the newspapers – as a potential threat to Mandela. This danger is not explicitly stated, but is still clearly expressed through the use of cinematic language.

Through careful placement of symbols and a focus on mise en scène, Eastwood presents a great deal of information to the audience. This begins right from the opening scenes, which clearly illustrate the disparity between the experiences of white and black school students. In addition, his use of symbols – such as the changing ratios of old and new South African flags – illustrates the gradual shift towards acceptance and reconciliation. When watching the film, it is important to pay close attention to everything in the shot, as this constitutes the language of film, and contributes a great deal to the meaning.

The soundtrack

As well as presenting information visually, Eastwood makes deliberate use of sound to express ideas and add to the film's drama. His use of diegetic and non-diegetic sound is worth paying particular attention to. Diegetic sound, which refers to sound that exists within the world of the film and can be heard by the characters, includes the use of the crowd booing, cheering and singing at the rugby matches, the television commentaries, and, although exaggerated, the grunts, groans and sounds of impact during the rugby scenes. This use of sound works to increase the audience's immersion in the film and adds to the sense of realism.

It provides Eastwood with an opportunity to convey information – for example, to show that Mandela was booed loudly on his early public appearances – without having to state this explicitly. Audiences are positioned to make their own judgements about the sounds they hear.

Not everything the audience hears is also heard by the characters in the film. Non-diegetic sound is sound that the audience can hear, but the characters within the film cannot. For example, when Mandela meets the Springboks during their final preparations for the World Cup (Scene 15) the song 'Colorblind', by South African band Overtone, plays in the background as Mandela gets out of the helicopter. The message imparted by this song is clear – colour should not make a difference – and the use of this song at this moment in the film allows Eastwood to emphasise Mandela's determination to create a rainbow nation.

Similarly, the voice-over of Mandela reciting 'Invictus' as the Springboks tour Robben Island Prison (Scene 17) encourages audiences to draw a connection between the poem's meaning and Mandela's experience. The focus on Pienaar during this scene further enhances the impact of the poem, suggesting that he too possesses an 'unconquerable soul'. This creates a strong symbolic connection between Mandela and Pienaar, emphasising the similarities between them.

Q Consider the ways different characters speak. Does their language indicate their position in society? What does their language and vocabulary reveal about their character?

Q Choose a scene and analyse it closely, focusing on cinematic technique. Make notes on the use of sound (both diegetic and non-diegetic), camera angles, lighting etc. How do these elements contribute to the meaning of the film? It may be useful to create a storyboard of your chosen scene.

SCENE-BY-SCENE ANALYSIS

Note that the numbered scenes or chapters identified on the DVD and below for navigation purposes typically include several scenes of the film. The time codes given here are approximate, as these can vary depending on the device and software used to play the DVD.

Scene 1

Summary: *Mandela's motorcade drives through the streets; a montage reveals de Klerk announcing Mandela's release from prison, followed by news footage that summarises the period between Mandela's release and his inauguration as president.*

The dichotomy between black and white South Africa is made obvious in the opening scene, which contrasts two schools – a privileged white boys' school and an obviously disadvantaged school for black students. While the black students crowd the fence and cheer as Mandela drives past, the white sports coach is critical of 'the terrorist Mandela', and warns his students that the release of Mandela will be remembered as the day the country 'went to the dogs'.

The subsequent montage reinforces this fear, focusing on riots and violence. The voice-over speaks ominously of the potential for 'a civil war', despite Mandela's plea that the weapons be thrown 'into the sea'. The scene ends with six military aircraft flying over the South African Government buildings, releasing trails of multi-coloured smoke – a representation of Mandela's plans for a rainbow nation.

Q How does Eastwood use visual elements to highlight the division between white and black South Africa?

Scene 2 (0:03:56)

Summary: *Mandela wakes early and goes for his regular morning walk; an erratically driven delivery van appears to be a threat, but proves to be harmless; newspaper headlines and a television announcer question Mandela's ability to lead; Mandela finds a bracelet in a drawer; Mr Pienaar expresses his fear about the new regime.*

Mandela gets up at 4am and immediately makes his bed – a subtle reminder of the self-discipline he acquired while in prison. When he goes outside he greets bodyguards Jason and Linga in Xhosa, establishing that he is multilingual. This becomes important later in the film, as it is his ability to communicate with everyone that helps him win over the white South African people.

When a van speeds towards them, Jason and Linga fear the worst, only to realise that it is simply delivering newspapers. Mandela translates the Afrikaans headline for the men – 'He can win an election, but can he run a country?' He responds mildly with 'It's a legitimate question', demonstrating his willingness to allow all people a voice.

Key point

Mandela's ability to speak several languages is instrumental in allowing him to break down the boundaries between the various ethnic groups in South Africa. His focus on the power of language is further demonstrated in his deliberate use of inclusive language, which draws those around him in to share his vision.

This scene concludes with a montage of people preparing for their day: a sunrise over the townships, breakfast preparations, and Mandela shaving. His calm demeanour is shaken briefly when he finds an old bracelet belonging to his ex-wife in a bathroom drawer, reminding audiences that his personal life has suffered as a result of his determination to unite South Africa. The final frames of Scene 2 show Francois Pienaar having breakfast with his parents. Pienaar's father expresses his fear that the black population will take jobs and drive the Afrikaners 'into the sea'.

Q The danger implied by the speeding newspaper delivery van can be seen as a metaphor for the threat the media poses for Mandela's regime. What is Eastwood suggesting about the power of the media?

Key vocabulary

Afrikaans: a language of southern Africa, derived from Dutch. It is spoken mostly by white Afrikaner South Africans.

Afrikaner: an Afrikaans-speaking white South African, particularly one descended from the Dutch settlers.

Xhosa: the language spoken by Xhosa people, the second-largest ethnic group in South Africa; Mandela is Xhosa.

Scene 3 (0:07:46)

Summary: *Mandela arrives at the Union Buildings to find the white office staff packing their belongings; he addresses them.*

When Mandela walks into the Union Buildings (the seat of government and the president's offices in Pretoria) and finds the staff preparing to leave, he asks Brenda to summon them all to a meeting. Mandela assures them, in Afrikaans, that '*wat is verby is verby* – the past is the past'. By the time he has finished speaking, the staff are nodding and smiling. This meeting illustrates the way Mandela is able to identify and address people's fears, paving the way to mutual understanding.

Q How does Mandela use language, both spoken and non-verbal, to assuage the fears of the Afrikaner staff? Why is this effective?

Scene 4 (0:10:52)

Summary: *Jason requests additional security staff; the new staff are white Special Branch police who have trained with the SAS, and who worked for de Klerk; Mandela explains that his bodyguard must reflect his vision for the rainbow nation.*

Jason and his team are startled when four Special Branch police report for duty as the presidential bodyguard. Jason expresses his concerns to Mandela, reminding the president that the Special Branch 'tried to kill' members of the ANC. Mandela acknowledges this, but states that 'reconciliation starts here' and asks Jason to try to work with them. The black and white security staff reluctantly start to cooperate to protect the president. Scenes 3 and 4 both demonstrate Mandela's ability to inspire people to overcome their prejudices by understanding that 'forgiveness ... removes fear'.

Key point

The conversation between Jason and Mandela outlines the basis for restorative justice, a process by which people on both sides of a dispute are encouraged to understand and empathise with each other. This acknowledgement of humanity on both sides makes it easier to forgive the past, move beyond the enmity, and find common ground. This is the heart of Mandela's strategy as he works to reconcile the people of South Africa.

Scene 5 (0:15:51)

Summary: *Mandela attends a rugby match; the racial divide is obvious as white fans support the Springboks, and black fans cheer for England; the Sports Minister tells Mandela the National Sports Executive plans to abolish the Springbok name and colours.*

Mandela walks out into the stadium to meet the teams, and is greeted with a combination of cheers and boos, representing the division within South Africa. He wishes each of the Springboks good luck, but Chester is the only player he is able to address by name. It is clear that the Springboks are outclassed by the English team. Mandela notes with some amusement that the black fans are supporting the English team, and describes how he used to support anyone playing against the Springboks when he was on Robben Island because 'it made the wardens very angry'.

The Sports Minister arrives late and tells Mandela there is 'strong support to drop the Springbok emblem and colours altogether'. While the minister is clearly happy that 'the green and gold' may soon become obsolete, the camera lingers on the thoughtful face of Mandela, who does not seem as pleased by this news.

Scene 6 (0:22:56)

Summary: *TV sports commentator Johan de Villiers criticises the team; Mary advises Mandela that his daughter has cancelled her planned visit; the National Sports Council votes to eliminate the Springbok name from national sport.*

Johan de Villiers is caustic in his criticism of the Springboks, and Eastwood shows the reactions of several people to de Villiers' attack. The Rugby President responds by deciding that 'somebody gets the axe', while Pienaar feels that the diatribe is directed at him personally. His girlfriend Nerine comforts Pienaar by pointing out that de Villiers is 'bitter because the Springboks were boycotted when he played', a clear reference to the wide ranging sanctions against South Africa during the apartheid era. Mandela seems to be struck by de Villiers' reference to 'the hallowed green and gold'. While Mandela is contemplating this, his servant Mary comes in and advises him that his daughter Zindzi called to cancel her visit. Mandela is clearly disappointed by this news, which serves to remind audiences of the personal struggles he still faces.

The gap in understanding between black and white South Africa is illustrated by the surprised reaction of a white church worker to Sipho's rejection of a Springbok jersey. The woman's black colleague explains that 'for them Springbok still represents apartheid'. This highlights the challenges faced by Mandela as he strives to unify the nation, and to change the cultural and symbolic meanings associated with the Springboks.

Another group seeking to change these meanings is the National Sports Council, which votes overwhelmingly to eliminate 'the colours, emblem and the name of the Springboks' as they are symbols of apartheid.

Scene 7 (0:27:48)

Summary: *Mandela learns of the NSC decision and goes to the meeting to ask the voters to reconsider their decision.*

Mandela knows that removing the Springbok name will alienate the Afrikaners, creating ever-deeper divisions and hostilities, and he speaks to the meeting to ask voters to reconsider. He explains that the 'enemy is no longer the Afrikaner', and asks the Council to 'surprise them with the compassion, with restraint and generosity' rather than indulging in 'petty revenge'. While the support for his proposal is not unanimous (indicative of the slow move towards reconciliation), the NSC agrees to reinstate the Springbok name. Mandela then explains to Brenda that, as the Afrikaners still control 'the police, the army, and the economy', without their support the bigger issues cannot be resolved.

Q Consider the different attitudes to the Springbok emblem, name and colours expressed by the Sports Minister, the Sports Council, the Afrikaners, the black community and Mandela. How do these attitudes reflect the challenges facing Mandela in his desire for a unified South Africa?

Scene 8 (0:35:10)

Summary: *Pienaar struggles to inspire the team; the bodyguards are starting to work together; Mandela travels the world representing the new South Africa; Mandela is troubled by his family issues.*

Pienaar feels the pressure of having to inspire his teammates. After yet another defeat, he challenges his team to savour the taste of defeat and promise 'never to taste it again'. This marks a turning point for the Springboks. Meanwhile Mandela's bodyguards work together as they discuss the gruelling schedule for Mandela's official visits to the United Nations, the United States and Japan, which are then shown as news footage watched by Mr and Mrs Pienaar.

On returning home Mandela resumes his daily walks. When Hendrick asks him about his family, Mandela states that his is a 'very large family – 42 million', then, clearly saddened, abandons his walk. This highlights the fact that, in many ways, Mandela has sacrificed his personal life for his country, and has instead become a father figure to the entire nation.

Key point

Mandela's reference to his 'very large family – 42 million' in this scene shows that he is a father figure to his people, even as he struggles to be a father to his biological children. This is reinforced by his warm and paternal approach to others, treating every person he meets with respect and dignity.

The next day Mandela is shown reading the newspaper headlines, which focus on a rising crime rate and falling economy. On turning to the sports pages, Mandela notes that Pienaar has retained the captaincy of the Springboks, and he is pleased by this.

Q Eastwood makes extensive use of news footage and newspaper headlines throughout this film. What is the impact of this? Why do you think Eastwood has chosen to present information in this way?

Scene 9 (0:39:14)

Summary: *Mandela is shocked by his pay; Pienaar is invited to tea with Mandela.*

Brenda gives Mandela his pay cheques (which he hasn't been collecting), and he is appalled by the amount. He announces that he will be donating a third of his pay to charity, and hopes other ministers will follow his lead. While the Pienaar family watches news of this on the television, Francois receives a phone call inviting him to tea with Mandela. His family are in awe, but Eunice asks him to tell Mandela that 'the bus service is very bad, and too expensive'.

Q What do the different responses of the Pienaar family and Eunice to Mandela's invitation reveal about the way they regard the President and his role?

Q What is the point of Hendrick's anecdote about the English toffee?

Scene 10 (0:43:38)

Summary: *Pienaar has afternoon tea with Mandela.*

Mandela's interest in everyone around him is confirmed by the way he greets Pienaar, enquiring about the player's recent ankle injury, as well as by his warm interaction with Mrs Brits, the tea lady. His interactions with these two contrasting individuals confirm Hendrick's comment about Mandela as he walked down the corridor with Pienaar in the previous scene: 'to him no-one's invisible'. Mandela is portrayed as very human, and his ability to interact with people of all levels is shown to be a powerful strength.

The conversation turns to leadership. The two men discover a common leadership style – to lead by example – as well as a common challenge – to inspire people to be 'better than they think they can be'. Mandela uses the inclusive 'we' to engage Pienaar, and to encourage him to develop his leadership further. He tells Pienaar of his reliance on a poem ('Invictus') during his time on Robben Island, and Pienaar reveals that he uses music to motivate his team on the way to a match. Both men recognise the power of words to inspire, and to help others realise that in order to achieve success 'we must all exceed our own expectations'. Francois later realises that Mandela is asking him to exceed his own expectations and 'win the World Cup'.

Q Read the poem 'Invictus'. How is it relevant to this moment in the film?

Scene 11 (0:49:11)

Summary: *A photo shoot with Mandela and his grandchildren highlights the tension between him and his daughter, Zindzi.*

Mandela interrupts a publicity-photo session to talk to Zindzi, who is clearly upset by the photo of Mandela and Pienaar on the front page of the newspaper. She tells Mandela that Pienaar 'looks like one of the policemen who forced us out of our house while you were in jail'. This statement reveals Zindzi's deep resentment of her father's efforts to reconcile the black and white communities of South Africa at the expense of his family. Mandela suggests that she 'criticises without understanding', which 'does not serve the nation'. Stung by this, Zindzi lashes out when Mandela asks her to return a bracelet to her mother.

Q Compare Zindzi's description of Pienaar with Jason's initial response to the Afrikaner security team in Scene 4. What do these attitudes reveal about the origins of the current tensions between black and white South Africans?

Scene 12 (0:51:04)

Summary: *Mandela meets with the Minister of Sport; the Springboks endure a gruelling training session; the head of South African Rugby tells the players they will be running coaching clinics.*

Mandela and the Minister discuss the structure of the World Cup, and Mandela sees the prospect of a billion viewers worldwide as 'a great opportunity'. Their conversation is inter-cut with footage of a gruelling training session for the Springboks, when the coach states that 'they may not be the most talented team in the world, but they're sure as hell going to be the fittest', foreshadowing their ultimate victory in the World Cup final as a result of their extraordinary stamina.

After training, the head of South African Rugby addresses the team and advises them that they are to conduct coaching clinics in townships all over the country, as part of the PR build-up to the World Cup. The players are unhappy at the prospect, but Pienaar recognises that the Springboks have 'become more than just a rugby team'. He tells the team that 'times change, and we need to change as well', revealing his trust in Mandela's judgement. Pienaar also mirrors Mandela's use of inclusive language.

Q Mandela and Pienaar both have to find ways to overcome resistance from those they lead. Summarise the similarities and differences in the challenges they face and their leadership styles.

Scene 13 (0:54:28)

Summary: *The Springboks run their first coaching clinic.*

As the Springboks' bus drives through the township, the men are visibly shocked by the level of poverty they observe. Although they are sceptical as they get off the bus, the men are soon won over by the positive energy of the children. Chester, as the first black Springbok, is an obvious crowd favourite, and the children chant 'Chester, Chester!' in the same way they chanted for Mandela in the opening scene. When the Springboks depart, they leave behind rugby balls, happy children, and a banner proclaiming 'ONE TEAM, ONE COUNTRY'. Mandela interrupts an official meeting to watch the television footage of the clinic, remarking that the images are 'worth any number of speeches'.

Q What is Mandela trying to achieve by sending the team to run coaching clinics in the townships? In your opinion, is this clinic successful?

Scene 14 (0:58:36)

Summary: *The Springboks arrive in Cape Town; de Villiers' comments reveal a softening in his attitude to the team; Mandela hand-writes a copy of the poem 'Invictus' for Pienaar; the security staff work together on security plans for the World Cup; Mandela memorises the names and faces of all the Springboks; Pienaar hands out the words to 'N'kosi Sikelel' iAfrika'.*

This fast-moving section builds tension across all of the storylines as the World Cup draws nearer. The Springboks are starting to function effectively as a team, shown by the synchronous way they exit the plane and conduct their training run. Even de Villiers pronounces himself to be 'cautiously optimistic' about the Springboks' chances. At the same time, Mandela's bodyguards are working well together to plan for the security challenge that is a major international sporting event. Mandela offers a gesture of support and encouragement to Pienaar by hand-writing a copy of 'Invictus' for him.

The only sour note in this section is the Springboks' response to Pienaar's request that they learn the Xhosa words to 'N'kosi Sikelel' iAfrica'. They are dismissive of the need to learn something they still regard as a 'terrorist song', particularly as they 'can't even read it, or pronounce the words'. Pienaar seems to back down, but as he leaves he tells the team, 'It means "God bless Africa", which, you have to admit, we could use'. Some team members nod in agreement, which suggests that, as with other change, support will come, albeit slowly.

Key point

'N'kosi Sikelel' iAfrika' was the official anthem for the African National Congress during the apartheid era, and was banned by the Afrikaner regime. It was adopted alongside the English-language anthem in 1994 and in 1997 the two were combined in a new South African national anthem, but many white South Africans struggled to accept a song that, to them, represented people they had been taught to regard as terrorists. This mirrors the black attitude to the Springboks, a team that for them represents apartheid and Afrikaner rule. Fear and mistrust exists on both sides, creating a challenge for Mandela as he attempts to eliminate the longstanding enmity.

Scene 15 (1:04:11)

Summary: *Mandela is interviewed by de Villiers on television; Mandela visits the Springboks and gives Pienaar the poem.*

This scene opens with de Villiers interviewing Mandela on the Topsport channel. The initial questions are posed in quite a supercilious tone, and de Villiers appears to be challenging Mandela's support of the Springboks. When he states that in the past Mandela was known to 'support any team that played against the Springboks', Mandela's response is to ask: 'if I cannot change when circumstances demand it, how can I expect others to?' While on the surface Mandela is referring to rugby, he uses this as an opportunity to remind the people of South Africa that they need to change their attitudes if the rainbow nation is to become a reality.

On the day before the match against Australia, Mandela visits the Springboks as they train. Pienaar is about to introduce the men when Mandela stops him, saying, 'I know who this is'. He then addresses most of the players by name, and the men are visibly pleased by the recognition. Mandela is disappointed to hear that Chester is injured. The team gives him a Springbok cap, which he is 'truly honoured' to accept. As he is leaving, Mandela gives Pienaar the copy of 'Invictus'. Pienaar understands the power of this gesture, telling Nerine that the poem is his 'inspiration'.

Scene 16 (1:09:25)

Summary: *The Springboks defeat Australia; the presidential bodyguard is working as a team.*

The action cuts between the rugby and Mandela's security team, suggesting that for both storylines this game is a climactic moment. The Springboks play well, and walk away victorious. At the same time the security guards form stronger connections, with Hendrick explaining the game to Jason as they watch together. The unity of the crowd as they celebrate the Springbok victory justifies Mandela's faith in the power of sport to bring people together. The chapter ends with a variety of celebrations.

Scene 17 (1:13:30)

Summary: *The Springboks visit Robben Island.*

The Springboks' training run ends at the waterfront, where their coach and partners are waiting for them on a ferry that will take them to

Robben Island, the prison where Mandela was held for nearly thirty years. As the team tours the prison, Pienaar is transfixed by visions of Mandela reading in his cell and breaking rocks in the yard. Mandela recites 'Invictus' in a voice-over, and the words are given particular gravitas in this setting.

Q What is achieved by Eastwood's use of flashbacks in this scene?

Q Why has Eastwood used 'Invictus' at this point in the film? What is the impact of having the poem recited as a voice-over in this scene?

Scene 18 (1:17:38)

Summary: *Mandela collapses from exhaustion and is confined to bed; Chester is declared fit to play; the Springboks progress through to the finals; Mandela continues to work; the security staff play rugby together.*

Hendrick and Jason arrive to escort Mandela on his morning walk, only to find he has collapsed. The doctor prescribes complete rest, not 'simply shifting the affairs of state to his bedroom'. This shows Mandela to be human, regardless of his incredible achievements. By placing this moment after Pienaar's trip to Robben Island, Eastwood emphasises the physical hardship Mandela has experienced throughout his life.

Meanwhile Chester is declared fit to play. The Springboks' teamwork is obvious as they progress through the next two matches. Mandela continues to work, despite his doctor's orders, and remains up to date with the Springboks' World Cup campaign. He clears his schedule to watch the game between England and the All Blacks, and the action cuts between Mandela and the Springboks, all watching the game and analysing the teams. The synchronicity between Mandela and the players shows how united they are in their common goal. While the game is on television, the security staff take a break and play rugby in Mandela's garden – a microcosm of what Mandela is striving for on a national level. He points this out to Brenda and asks, 'still think I'm wasting my time with the rugby?' (Scene 18).

Q Why is it so important that Chester plays as part of the Springboks team?

Scene 19 (1:25:09)

Summary: *Pienaar gives his family and Eunice tickets to the World Cup final; the Minister of Sport briefs Mandela on the All Blacks; an unidentified man visits the stadium; Pienaar reflects on Mandela's life; Jason and Etienne complete a final check of stadium security.*

Pienaar presents his family with four tickets to the final. He has included Eunice, demonstrating his own changed attitude to the black people around him and gently challenging his father to do the same. The Minister of Sport's briefing emphasises just how big a challenge the Springboks face in their match against the All Blacks, and Mandela expresses the importance of victory, because South Africa is 'hungry for greatness'.

An unidentified man walks into Ellis Park Stadium, accompanied by ominous music. This adds tension to the scene, as he appears to be scoping out the grounds.

The night before the match Pienaar states that 'tomorrow's taken care of'; while he is referring specifically to the rugby match, this also applies to the lasting legacy Mandela created for South Africa. Pienaar contemplates 'how you spend thirty years in a tiny cell, and come out ready to forgive the people who put you there'. At the same time Etienne and Jason are checking security measures one last time, illustrating their unity in pursuing a common goal.

Scene 20 (1:28:37)

Summary: *The morning of the grand final; a plane flies very low over the stadium.*

Everyone is shown completing their own preparations for the day. The Springboks run through the streets of Johannesburg and are cheered by fans of all colours. Jason briefs the security team. The film cuts immediately to a view of the stadium through binoculars, and then reveals the viewer to be the same mysterious man who was scoping out the stadium the day before. The music again creates tension.

Crowds of fans, including Sipho, descend on the stadium, waving Springbok and new South African flags. A voice-over by de Villiers explains that the crowd is 'at fever pitch' because 'their beloved green and gold has somehow managed to defy all expectations'. The scene shifts from the packed stadium to an SAA (South African Airways) aeroplane flying above Johannesburg. The mysterious man is the pilot, and he makes an unscheduled low pass over the stadium, revealing the words 'GOOD LUCK BOKKE' (Springboks) painted on the underside.

Q Note de Villiers' reference to 'their beloved green and gold'. How does this contrast with the attitudes expressed in Scene 6?

Scene 21 (1:33:40)

Summary: *The teams run onto the field; Mandela walks onto the field wearing Pienaar's number 6 jersey and a Springbok cap; national pride is high.*

This scene is the culmination of the work done by Pienaar and Mandela. The stadium is filled with South African fans all cheering for the Springboks, and crowds of both black and white people are gathered around every available television. The Springboks sing along with 'N'kosi Sikelel' iAfrika', sending a powerful message of unity to the nation.

Key point

Mandela's wearing of the Springbok jersey and cap can be seen as a physical extension of his frequent use of inclusive language. With this obvious demonstration of support for, and identification with, the Springboks, Mandela sends a clear message to the world that the team represents all of South Africa. This powerful gesture reinforces the 'One team, one country' message, and elevates the Springboks to a South African team rather than an Afrikaner one.

Scene 22 (1:39:59)

Summary: *Mandela and the New Zealand Prime Minister agree to a wager; the All Blacks perform the haka; the game begins; Sipho, left outside the stadium, lingers near a police car trying to hear the match on their radio; people all around the country are shown watching the match on television at home and in public places.*

The soundtrack for the match scenes (Scenes 22–5) emphasises the umpire's whistle and the grunts and sounds of impact between the players, accompanied by a pervasive African drum beat, giving these scenes a primal feel. As the mood intensifies the editing changes pace. Increasingly frequent crosscutting between the VIP box, the players, the crowd, the scoreboard, the security men, Zindzi and her family, the Pienaar family, and the crowds gathered in bars and homes around South Africa emphasises the fact that every South African appears to be hoping for the same thing – a Springbok victory. This bodes well for Mandela's vision of the rainbow nation.

Scene 23 (1:48:19)

Summary: *As the game progresses, Sipho gets closer to the police car, until he is listening with them.*

As the game continues, Sipho, who has remained outside the stadium, gradually moves closer to the police car. After initially shooing Sipho away, the police relent and allow him to listen with them. The developing ease between Sipho and authority figures symbolises the improving relationships between black and white South Africans.

Scene 24 (1:48:32)

Summary: *The game has to go into extra time; when the crowd starts to sing, Pienaar addresses his players once more, beseeching them to listen to their country; the Springboks win the match.*

When he realises that the match will go into extra time, Pienaar asks his players 'who's the fittest team on this field?' When, as the volume of the Springbok supporters' singing increases, he urges them 'Listen to your country', he mirrors Mandela's use of inclusive language, encouraging the players to identify with the nation.

Scene 25 (1:53:17)

Summary: *The Springboks win the match; the team forms a final huddle and Chester leads them in a prayer; black and white spectators embrace each other; the policemen and Sipho celebrate together.*

The final moments of the match are presented in slow motion, both in terms of the soundtrack and the camerawork. This has the effect of emphasising every impact, as well as increasing the level of tension. The final kick feels agonisingly slow, and the last thirty seconds of the game are filled with primal grunts, groans and roars. When the Springboks win and the film speed returns to normal, the jubilation of the crowd feels even more exultant in contrast with the slow-motion scenes.

Amid the joy, the Springboks take a final moment to be together as a team, forming a huddle. In the relative calm Pienaar asks Chester to lead the team in a prayer.

Q The crowd's singing is instrumental in motivating the team. Identify other instances in the film where singing and music are shown to be powerful inspirations. What do these moments have in common?

Scene 26 (1:57:25)

Summary: *Scenes of jubilation follow; de Villiers interviews Pienaar on the field; Mandela presents the trophy to Pienaar; Sipho is given a cap by a policeman. Fans throng the city streets; Mandela leaves the stadium and is caught up in the crowds; he relaxes as he journeys back home; there is a voice-over refrain of 'Invictus'.*

As the players separate, de Villiers approaches and speaks to Pienaar, who echoes Mandela's words from earlier in the film and acknowledges 'the support of 43 million South Africans'. When Mandela presents the trophy to Pienaar, both men recognise and acknowledge the service the other has done for their country.

The final scene shows extensive celebrations, with crowds of people dancing in the streets. The security guards are all in two cars, with the racial divide completely eliminated. Mandela advises his team that there is 'no hurry at all', and he sits back to enjoy the celebrations of his rainbow nation.

Q Sipho treasures the cap given to him by an Afrikaner policeman, yet in an earlier scene he rejected a Springbok rugby jumper. Describe the transformation in Sipho's attitude. To what extent does Sipho's journey mirror the journey of all black South Africans?

Scene 27 (2:01:23)

Summary: *Credits.*

The final credits roll, showing photos taken during the World Cup final. This serves to emphasise the fact that the story of *Invictus* is a true one.

Q Look closely at the final two scenes. How does Eastwood use visual elements to suggest Mandela has indeed created a rainbow nation?

CHARACTERS AND RELATIONSHIPS

Nelson Mandela

Key quotes

'The rainbow nation starts here. Reconciliation starts here ... Forgiveness starts here too.' (Scene 4)

'You elected me your leader. Let me lead you now.' (Scene 7)

'I will do what I must to stop that cycle. Or it will destroy us.' (Scene 7)

'I have a very large family – 42 million.' (Scene 8)

'If I cannot change when circumstances demand it, how can I expect others to?' (Scene 15)

Nelson Mandela, born on 18 July 1918, is the central character in *Invictus*. The film commences with his release from prison, where he has been for twenty-seven years. At the age of seventy-two he could reasonably be expected to retire from public life. Instead he chooses to remain in the political arena. His election as president comes four years after his release, and he is faced with the daunting task of leading a country on the brink of civil war. The dismantling of apartheid has left the Afrikaner population feeling vulnerable, while many black citizens are calling for revenge. Mandela has to address the concerns of all South Africans and balance 'black aspirations with white fears' (Scene 2) if he is to stabilise the nation.

Mandela's personal suffering under apartheid is alluded to quite subtly by Eastwood. His sensitivity to light, caused by years of hard labour in the glare of full sun on Robben Island, is hinted at (Scene 10); similarly, his collapse due to exhaustion (Scene 18) reminds the audience of his age and his difficult life. In addition, the toll his incarceration and political activism has taken on his family life is evident in his estrangement from his wife Winnie and the strained relationship he has with Zindzi, the only daughter mentioned in the film. As Linga points out to Hendrick, 'he's separated from his wife' (Scene 8) and his children rarely visit. Mandela's family has paid a high price for his life in the public and political arena.

The extraordinary thing about Nelson Mandela is his astonishing capacity for forgiveness. Despite his ill treatment at the hands of the Afrikaner government, Mandela leaves jail 'ready to forgive' (Scene 19) the people who put him there. As Mandela tells Jason, 'forgiveness liberates the soul. It removes fear. That is why it is such a powerful weapon' (Scene 4). He realises that the only way to rebuild South Africa and create his 'rainbow nation' is through reconciliation, and he chooses sport as the medium through which to unite the people. His ability to recognise the power of sport to bring disparate groups together demonstrates his creative and innovative approach to leadership. Mandela encounters resistance from his staff, his family and his supporters, but he has faith in the path he has chosen, and his faith is ultimately shown to be well placed.

In addition to his creative yet clear-headed approach, Mandela also models the behaviour he seeks to inspire in others. One of his first acts as president is to show acceptance and forgiveness towards the Afrikaner staff in his offices, personally asking them to stay and do their country 'a great service' (Scene 3). This sets the tone for his leadership; because he is seen to be capable of forgiveness himself, he is able to ask the same of others. He reminds the people that they must 'look to the future now' (Scene 3). When Mandela asks the National Sports Council to retain the Springbok name and colours, or asks Jason Tshabalala to work with the Afrikaner security team, people accept his leadership despite their initial doubts, because they know he is not asking of them anything that he would not do himself. They realise that he has the moral authority to ask these things of others.

One of Mandela's greatest strengths is his ability to communicate on an equal footing with everybody. Mandela's ability to speak with people and put them at ease is crucial to his success as a leader and he is shown interacting comfortably with a wide variety of individuals, from rugby fans in the stadium to international leaders, both Afrikaner and black staff, and the world media. As Hendrick expresses it, 'To him no-one's invisible' (Scene 9).

Mandela is equally comfortable addressing a large crowd. His inauguration speech passionately asks that South Africa never again 'experience the oppression of one by another, and suffer the indignity of being the skunk of the world' (Scene 1), clearly indicating from the first days of his presidency that he seeks reconciliation rather than revenge. Even when he is making unpopular decisions, people are prepared to trust his guidance, which is a mark of a great leader. His willingness to make not only political calculations but also 'a human calculation' (Scene 7) allows him to guide his country towards reconciliation.

Francois Pienaar

Key quotes

'We've become more than just a rugby team, and we might as well get used to it.' (Scene 12)

'Times change, and we need to change as well.' (Scene 12)

'Tomorrow's taken care of, one way or another.' (Scene 19)

'Do you hear? Listen to your country. This is our destiny.' (Scene 24)

Francois Pienaar, captain of the Springboks rugby team, comes from a conservative Afrikaner family. He has been raised in an apartheid society, and his father in particular is wary of Mandela's presidency. Unexpectedly, Pienaar does not appear to hold his father's racist views. He is surprised and nervous when he is invited to have afternoon tea with Mandela, but this appears to be because of Pienaar's awe for Mandela's position rather than an indication of any racism. Indeed, when Pienaar meets Mandela he quickly warms to the President as they share their convergent views on leadership and inspiration.

Pienaar is in the difficult position of leading a team that has not been tried on the world stage due to the international boycott of apartheid South Africa. In this way his position is similar to Mandela's –

both are leading their followers into unfamiliar territory, and both have the eyes of the world on them. The Springboks are dismissed by commentators as being 'utterly unprepared to re-enter the world of top-notch international rugby' (Scene 6), in the same way that Mandela was challenged by doubting newspaper headlines that asked 'can he run a country?' (Scene 2). Each man faces resistance to his leadership. Both overcome this resistance by remaining true to their ideals, and by leading 'by example' (Scene 10), not asking anything of their followers that they are not prepared to do themselves.

With Mandela's support and guidance Pienaar develops confidence in his leadership. He is able to inspire his team to support his decisions, even when these decisions are initially unpopular. Pienaar embraces Mandela's vision of the Springboks as a unifying force, and he works hard to convince his teammates to embrace their new role as 'more than just a rugby team' (Scene 12). His support of the township coaching clinics and his willingness to learn the new South African national anthem even though it is regarded by some of the Springboks as 'their bloody song, not ours' (Scene 14), illustrates his determination to rise to the challenge set by Mandela – to 'win the World Cup' (Scene 10). His positive approach, accompanied by his ability to influence his teammates, helps his team achieve success.

Key point

The relationship between Mandela and Pienaar is the central one in this film. Mandela acts as a mentor to Pienaar, teaching him how to be an effective leader. Their first meaningful encounter, when Pienaar has afternoon tea with Mandela, sets the tone for the rest of their interactions throughout the film. The mutual respect is evident as they discuss their common approach to leadership, both preferring to lead 'by example' (Scene 10).

Mandela gently guides Pienaar to become an even more effective leader by demonstrating how to interact with others in a positive way, modelling this when he treats Mrs Brits, the elderly tea lady, with courtesy and respect despite their difference in status. Pienaar recognises the power of Mandela's inclusive approach, mirroring it when he invites Eunice to attend the World Cup final with his parents and fiancée. Similarly, Pienaar takes inspiration from 'N'kosi Sikelel' iAfrica' in the same way that Mandela did at the 1992 Olympic Games, with both men realising that sometimes the best words are 'the work of others' (Scene 10).

The mutual admiration between the men is most clearly expressed in the final moments of the film, when Mandela presents Pienaar with the World Cup trophy. When Mandela thanks Pienaar for what he has done 'for our country', Pienaar responds by saying, 'Mr President, thank you for what you have done' (Scene 26). Both men acknowledge the impact of the other, and both realise that together they have achieved something extraordinary.

Brenda Mazibuko

Key quotes

'Do you see all those old apartheid flags? They're a disgrace ... It's time people moved on.' (Scene 5)

'You're risking your political capital ... At least risk it for something more important than rugby.' (Scene 7)

Brenda Mazibuko is President Mandela's chief of staff, and also functions as his closest advisor. While most women in the film work within the domestic sphere, Brenda's authority in the political and economic realm is significant. She frequently appears to be frustrated by Mandela's attitude towards rugby, and struggles to understand why he would risk his 'political capital' (Scene 7) for a game played by 'thugs' (Scene 14). By political capital Brenda means the level of trust and goodwill Mandela has built up with the public and with other politicians, both locally and globally. She is concerned that he may lose some of this goodwill if he is seen to be obsessed with sport instead of governance. Brenda's own political focus is on 'housing, food, jobs, crime ... currency', and she sees Mandela's interest in rugby as a distraction designed to 'placate a minority' (Scene 7) while ignoring the bigger problems. Mandela gently reminds Brenda that the minority in question (the Afrikaners) still control 'the police, the army and the economy, and if we lose them we cannot address the other issues' (Scene 7). His biggest challenge is 'balancing black aspirations with white fears' (Scene 2), and he identifies sport, particularly rugby, as a means of achieving this goal.

Brenda remains resistant until she observes the friendly rugby game played between Mandela's black and Afrikaner security staff, which forces her to acknowledge the unifying power of the game and recognise that Mandela was not 'wasting [his] time with the rugby' (Scene 18). Brenda is protective of Mandela, but remains focused on the governance of South Africa. She understands the mood of the people, and Eastwood uses her character to represent the opinions of moderate black South Africa. While she understands Mandela's desire for unity, she is sometimes mystified by his strategy, reflecting the opinion of many South Africans of the time.

Jason Tshabalala and Linga Moonsamy

Key quotes

'Seriously. It's the new South Africa.' (Linga, Scene 4)

'He saw it. He sees everything.' (Jason, Scene 5)

'I just want to get him through tomorrow safely. That's all.' (Jason, Scene 19)

Jason, Linga and the other black members of Mandela's security team have worked with Mandela (whom they address as Madiba, his clan name and a mark of great respect), for many years. They are fiercely protective of the President who, for them, represents hope and growing equality. Their pride is clearly shown when the men walk into the Union Buildings on Mandela's first day in office – the satisfaction on Linga's face when he sees a portrait of Mandela being hung on the wall is evident.

Jason and Linga struggle to accept Mandela's dedication to the ideal of reconciliation. Jason asks Mandela to reconsider the decision to hire Afrikaner bodyguards because he finds it difficult to forgive men who 'not long ago … tried to kill' (Scene 4) black South Africans. Mandela is understanding but firm in his insistence that the bodyguard must represent 'the rainbow nation', and Jason agrees to work with the Afrikaners while still finding it impossible to 'trust them' (Scene 4). Jason represents the fears of a country struggling to overcome the legacy of apartheid; while he embraces the abolition of the divisive regime, he is challenged by the dramatic changes this entails.

Jason, Linga and the other members of Mandela's black security team maintain their separation from the Afrikaner guards by referring to Mandela as Madiba, emphasising to Etienne 'that's what *we* call him' (Scene 4). The emphasis placed on the word 'we' clearly identifies this as a point of difference between the guards, a difference further emphasised by the fact that Jason and Linga address Mandela in Xhosa. Their journey towards reconciliation mirrors that of many South Africans, being a challenging process that is only made possible by their acceptance of a common goal – in this case, to protect the President.

Etienne Feyder and Hendrick Booyens

Key quotes

'We'll call him Mr President.' (Etienne, Scene 4)

'To him no-one's invisible.' (Hendrick, Scene 9)

Etienne Feyder, Hendrick Booyens and the other Afrikaner security guards are experienced military men who used to protect de Klerk, the previous president. They represent the old regime, and for Jason and his team their arrival is very confronting. The Afrikaner guards initially hold themselves apart from Jason's team, speaking to each other in Afrikaans and making little effort to join forces. Over time, however, it becomes evident that all men share the common purpose of protecting the President, and as they work together to achieve this they learn to overcome their personal differences. Their struggle reflects that of the wider community, with old enmities proving difficult to put aside.

Key point

When Jason Tshabalala expresses a need for more security staff, Mandela responds by appointing 'four Special Branch cops' (Scene 4), including Etienne Feyder and Hendrick Booyens. Jason and his team find this challenging, but Mandela insists that his bodyguards represent him, and as such must reflect 'the rainbow nation'. The long journey from distrust to a friendly game of rugby represents the challenges faced by all South Africans as they put aside their differences and find common ground through sport.

Chester Williams

Key quote

'I try not to think, 'cause it interferes with my rugby.' (Scene 12)

Chester is a rare example of a black South African who has found success in the traditionally white-dominated sport of rugby. As the only black member of the Springboks, he provides a focus for reconciliation, symbolising the opening up of traditionally white arenas. While Mandela bemoans the fact that 'Chester is far too easy to identify' (Scene 14), he still provides hope for the success of the rainbow nation. He becomes the face of the Springboks for black South Africans; he is treated as a hero when the Springboks run a coaching clinic in an impoverished township, and a South African Airways plane is emblazoned with his image. Chester does not seem to be entirely comfortable with the spotlight, but as the only black member of the team he has little choice but to embrace his role as a symbol of reconciliation and unification.

Mr and Mrs Pienaar

Key quote

'They're going to take our jobs and they're going to drive us into the sea.' (Scene 2)

Francois Pienaar's parents are very conservative middle-class white South Africans. Mr Pienaar, in particular, is worried by the new regime, fearing that, under Mandela, black South Africans will seek revenge for years of apartheid. His fears have some historic precedent, which he refers to when he tells Pienaar to 'look at Angola, look at Mozambique. Look at Zimbabwe' (Scene 2). All of these countries experienced civil unrest when their white governments lost power to the black majority. Mr Pienaar's scepticism about Mandela's government is shown in his cynical response to the Mandela-related news items he sees on television.

Mr and Mrs Pienaar represent the 'white fears' alluded to in the opening montage, and their journey towards acceptance mirrors that of many South Africans. Over time they come to regard Eunice, their black maid, with increasing respect, and she attends the Rugby World Cup final with them. They also learn to embrace Mandela's vision of the rainbow nation, and this is particularly clear when the audience sees Mr Pienaar singing the new national anthem, including the verses written in African languages, at the final.

Zindzi

Key quote

> 'I think he looks like one of the policemen who forced us out of our house while you were in jail. I don't like seeing you shake his hand. And I'm not the only one.' (Scene 11)

Zindzi is one of two daughters born to Nelson and Winifred (Winnie) Mandela. Her body language reveals her emotional distance from her father; Eastwood also emphasises the separation between father and daughter by first showing her positioned in a doorway just outside the room Mandela is in. Zindzi cancels scheduled visits to Mandela (Scene 6), and refuses to act as a go-between when Mandela asks her to return a bracelet to her mother. Mandela's interactions with his daughter are awkward and uncomfortable, in stark contrast to his ability to relate warmly to everyone else he encounters. He berates her for her 'selfish thinking' that 'does not serve the nation' (Scene 11), which illustrates for the audience the source of their antagonism. It is clear from this exchange that Mandela's primary focus is the nation, and Zindzi has probably always felt that this was at the expense of his family.

Despite Zindzi's dislike of Pienaar (or rather, what Pienaar represents to her), and regardless of her difficult relationship with Mandela, Zindzi is shown with a group of people watching the World Cup final on television. Her pleasure in the Springboks' victory is clearly evident, albeit restrained. Through this Eastwood suggests that even those most resistant to reconciliation are caught up in the moment, which endorses Mandela's decision to use sport as a way to unify the nation.

THEMES, IDEAS & VALUES

Communication: the power of language and symbols

Key quotes

'Thank you for honouring our new flag.' (Mandela, Scene 5)

'For twenty-seven years I studied them. I learned their language, read their books, their poetry. I had to know my enemy before I could prevail against him.' (Mandela, Scene 7)

'A Victorian poem. Just words. But they helped me to stand when all I wanted was to lie down.' (Mandela, Scene 10)

'We need to learn this song. We can't just mouth the words anymore.' (Pienaar, Scene 14)

'It's their bloody song, not ours.' (Springbok player, Scene 14)

Invictus demonstrates Nelson Mandela's talent for communication, using both verbal and non-verbal means to convey his ideas. He frequently demonstrates his ability to find the right words to suit the situation. He is aided in this by the fact that he is multilingual, which allows him to speak directly to people rather than relying on translators. Mandela is able to ease the fears of the largely Afrikaner staff in the Union Buildings by addressing them in Afrikaans; similarly, he uses Xhosa to communicate with his black security team, and English when he addresses the international audience of the United Nations. By using the language of the people he is communicating with, Mandela effectively removes one of the barriers to communication, making it much more likely that people will hear his message. He further reduces barriers through his deliberate use of body language and eye contact, and through his refusal to hide 'behind men with guns' (Scene 3).

Key point

Note that communication goes beyond the written or spoken word – Mandela's use of body language and symbols is as effective as the words he uses.

Mandela is very deliberate in his use of the words of others. His championing of the Xhosa anthem 'N'kosi Sikelel' iAfrica' demonstrates his understanding of the power and meaning of this anthem for black South Africans. The song was the unofficial anthem of the ANC, the anti-apartheid movement denounced under the old regime as a terrorist organisation. By making it a second national anthem (and later incorporating into a new national anthem lyrics written in the five most widely spoken official languages of South Africa – Xhosa, Zulu, Sesotho, Afrikaans and English), Mandela presents a clear symbol of unity and equality. The energy and enthusiasm with which the crowd, and the Springboks, sing this anthem at the World Cup final demonstrates the effectiveness of the anthem as a unifying force; indeed, Pienaar draws on the song's inspirational quality in his final team address in the dying minutes of the game, exhorting his team to 'listen to your country' (Scene 24). This is in stark contrast to the team's initial response to Pienaar's suggestion that they learn the words, when most team members refuse on the basis that 'it's a terrorist song' and they 'can't even read it, or pronounce the words' (Scene 14).

While Mandela uses the anthem to inspire others, he also draws inspiration from William Ernest Henley's poem 'Invictus'. He explains to Pienaar that, even though the poem is 'just words' (Scene 10), it gave him the strength to go on while he was in jail. Mandela hand-writes a copy of the poem to give Pienaar, hoping that he will be similarly inspired.

In addition to verbal communication, Mandela uses symbols deliberately to share his message. He introduces new symbols, such as the new South African flag, to demonstrate new beginnings and reconciliation, while he is also able to reframe existing symbols – such as the Springbok name, logo and colours – so that they come to represent unity rather than apartheid. As he explains to the National Sports Council, 'this is the time to build our nation using every single brick available to us – even if that brick comes wrapped in green and gold' (Scene 7). In the same way that Mandela encourages white South Africans to accept 'N'kosi Sikelel' iAfrica', he asks black South Africans to embrace the Springboks. By ensuring elements from both white and black cultures are assigned universal relevance, Mandela gives all citizens an opportunity to achieve reconciliation through blending the familiar and the less familiar. The purposeful use of language, words and symbols is central to Mandela's efforts to unify his nation.

Q Many symbols change their meaning throughout the film as Mandela deliberately redefines them. Draw up and complete the table below to summarise the way symbols change over the course of the film. Try to include quotes and references to specific moments in the film. The first one has been done to give you some guidance.

Symbol	Early example and meaning	Later example and meaning	What is suggested by this change?
Springbok jersey	Sipho refuses to accept a Springbok jersey from a church group because it represents apartheid.	Mandela wears a Springbok jersey onto the field before and after the World Cup final.	The jersey, which used to epitomise apartheid, has been transformed into a symbol of a united South Africa.
South African flags			
South African anthem			
Rugby/ Springboks			
Robben Island			

Leadership, power and authority

Key quotes

'In this instance the people are wrong. And as their elected leader it is my job to show them that.' (Mandela, Scene 7)

'You elected me your leader. Let me lead you now.' (Mandela, Scene 7)

Brenda: 'You're risking your future as our leader.'
Mandela: 'The day I am afraid to do that is the day I am no longer fit to lead.' (Scene 7)

On Mandela's first day in office the newspaper headlines ask, 'He can win an election, but can he run a country?' (Scene 2). This illustrates the challenge Mandela faces, as he has won the support of the majority but is yet to demonstrate his ability to inspire all citizens to work together to achieve a common goal. As president, Mandela is in the difficult position of having to make some unpopular decisions as he guides his country towards reconciliation. The true test of his leadership is how he manages these moments, as he must inspire others to follow him even if they find the direction he takes challenging. He recognises that sometimes making an unpopular decision might risk his 'political capital' (Scene 7), but believes that his personal integrity and the future of South Africa are more important than making decisions that simply pander to public opinion.

Mandela establishes his leadership style very quickly. His first act as president is to overcome the apprehension of the mainly white office workers in the Union Buildings. He arrives to find that many of the white staff are packing their belongings in the assumption that they will lose their jobs under a black president. Mandela addresses them directly, without 'hiding behind men with guns' (Scene 3). He acknowledges their fears without belittling them, and advises them that 'your language, or the colour of your skin, or who you worked for before' does not disqualify them from staying and doing their country 'a great service' (Scene 3). Eastwood's focus on the workers shows that while the staff are initially defensive, with lowered eyes and crossed arms, by the time Mandela has finished speaking they are more open, relieved and smiling. This small moment illustrates Mandela's leadership. He acknowledges people's fears and concerns directly, and mitigates these fears through calm and inclusive language.

Mandela is faced with a reversal of this situation when he addresses the National Sports Council, an organisation with its origins in the ANC. While the white Union Buildings staff were fearful, the NSC is vengeful. The meeting has just voted unanimously to abolish 'the colours, emblem and the name of the Springboks' as 'a permanent symbol of the apartheid era' (Scene 6). Mandela has the challenging task of overturning this decision, and he does so using an approach similar to that he applied in his office. He recognises and names the fears of the NSC, acknowledging that he is asking council members to put aside 'a moment's petty revenge' in order to 'surprise ... with compassion, with restraint and generosity' (Scene 7). While the body language of his audience implies resistance at first, Mandela is able to overcome this once again through his use of inclusive language and compassion.

Francois Pienaar's leadership of the Springboks initially appears to be quite shaky. During the Springboks' match against England Pienaar tries to inspire his team, but it is clear that he is not getting through to the players (Scene 5). The team's lack of success draws negative attention from the sports media, and Pienaar is lucky to hold on to his captain's role. When Mandela decides to use the Springboks as a focus for national pride and meets with Pienaar to get his support, Pienaar is inspired to unite his team and lead the Springboks to become a symbol of unity and reconciliation for South Africa. He achieves this by using similar strategies to Mandela – using inclusive language to create a common goal, leading by example, and acknowledging fears and resistance while still having a clear expectation that those fears can be overcome.

Eastwood suggests that leadership is not always about being popular, nor is it about doing exactly what people say they want. Rather, successful leadership is shown to depend on empathy and a clear vision. Both Mandela and Pienaar are able to lead because they know where they are taking their followers, and they have faith in the value of that destination. Mandela recognises that the road to reconciliation will require him to make difficult and sometimes unpopular decisions, but he is able to do so because he is unwavering in his goal. Similarly Pienaar is a more successful Springboks team captain once he has a clear direction and focus.

The capacity to change

Key quotes

'*Wat is verby is verby*. What is past is past. We look to the future now.' (Mandela, Scene 3)

'Times change, and we need to change as well.' (Pienaar, Scene 12)

'If I cannot change when circumstances demand it, how can I expect others to?' (Mandela, Scene 15)

One of the main recurring themes in *Invictus* is the challenge of overcoming a difficult past, particularly when this requires dramatic change. It is clear from the opening moments of the film that South Africa's apartheid past has left a lasting impact, illustrated by the privileged white rugby players playing on carefully groomed lawns across the road from an impoverished and poorly resourced school where black students play an unstructured game of soccer. The segregation between black and white South Africans may no longer be enshrined in law, but the years of fear and mistrust are not easily overcome. This is shown in many ways throughout the film: black and white staff are hesitant to work together; Sipho refuses to accept a Springbok jersey because 'the Springbok still represents apartheid' (Scene 6); there remains enormous inequality in the relative standards of living; Boers continue to wave the apartheid flag; and the Springboks resist Pienaar's request that they learn the new national anthem. All of these examples demonstrate the need for substantial change if the country is to find peace and stability.

Mandela uses a combination of strategies to implement change. He encourages those in his immediate circle to change their attitudes by putting them in positions where those attitudes must be addressed. An example of this is when he instructs four Afrikaner presidential guards to work with his black security team. The initial distrust and enmity is eventually overcome, and the security staff unite in their desire to protect Mandela, even though they persist in addressing him by different names. The transformation is not complete, and the two groups retain their own cultural identity, but they find enough common ground to work together, respect each other, and play an informal game of rugby on the presidential lawn. This bodes well for reconciliation on a larger scale.

Mandela strives to institute national change by uniting South Africa behind the Springboks rugby team. He seizes the opportunity provided by the World Cup to force black and white South Africans to reassess their attitudes towards each other. The white South African minority must overcome the prejudice inculcated in them by years of apartheid, learning to treat all citizens as equal. At the same time, black communities have to put aside any desire for 'petty revenge' and instead embrace their former oppressors as 'partners in democracy' (Scene 7). Mandela recognises the power of sport to encourage unity and patriotism, and thus sets his sights on the Springboks as a focus for his 'rainbow nation'. He understands that people will only change if there is a reason to do so, and are unlikely to change spontaneously without purpose and inspiration. By encouraging South Africans to embrace the Springboks, Mandela provides an impetus for change, giving them a common interest and paving the way for lasting reconciliation.

Q Write a paragraph on each of the central characters in the film, identifying how they have changed throughout the text. Find evidence to support your discussion, and make specific notes on how Eastwood makes the transformation clear to the audience.

Forgiveness and reconciliation

Key quotes

'Forgiveness liberates the soul. It removes fear. That is why it is such a powerful weapon.' (Mandela, Scene 4)

'You seek only to address your own personal feelings. That is selfish thinking, Zindzi. It does not serve the nation.' (Mandela to Zindzi, Scene 11)

'I'm thinking about how you spend thirty years in a tiny cell, but come out ready to forgive the people who put you there.' (Pienaar, Scene 19)

The opening scenes of *Invictus* clearly demonstrate the need for reconciliation. Eastwood uses a montage to summarise the four years between Mandela's release from prison and his election as president, and this reveals scenes of violence and unrest as well as scenes of jubilation. The film quickly establishes the disparity between black and white South Africa, and also reveals the continuing tension. A white rugby coach is heard to tell his team that the day Mandela is released from prison is 'the day our country went to the dogs', while at the same time black children across the road are cheering Mandela's motorcade. Reconciliation seems to be a long way away.

Mandela's most powerful tool in the struggle to unify South Africa is his own story and actions. His experiences under the oppressive apartheid rule are known to all South Africans, and Pienaar speaks for many when he wonders how, after twenty-seven years of hard labour, Mandela was able to 'come out ready to forgive' (Scene 19) those who put him there. Mandela's ability to look beyond the past and seek to build a rainbow nation inspires others, most of whom have less to forgive. While the Afrikaner population braces itself to be driven 'into the sea' (Scene 2), Mandela tells them to 'have no such fear' (Scene 3). He realises that he must set the tone for 'the new South Africa' (Scene 4), which is why he stresses to Jason that 'Forgiveness liberates the soul. It removes fear. That is why it is such a powerful weapon' (Scene 4).

Mandela is able to draw on both political and personal authority to insist that others accept his vision for a united nation. His election as president forces the white population to acknowledge his authority, and the dismantling of apartheid makes it illegal for them to continue to subjugate the black population. This understandably makes them afraid, as they expect Mandela and the black majority to seek revenge for the years of segregation and oppression. However, Mandela does not want to continue the cycle of revenge and retribution. Instead he tells Brenda, 'I will do what I must to stop that cycle. Or it will destroy us' (Scene 7). He does this by meeting antipathy and fear with forgiveness and compassion, disarming the wary Afrikaner population and paving the way for restorative conversations.

Not everyone supports Mandela's strategy. Brenda is initially sceptical, pointing out that 'the people want this' (Scene 7) when the National Sports Council votes to abolish the Springboks. She comes to appreciate Mandela's approach when she observes the unifying power of rugby as she watches the black and white security teams play a game together.

Zindzi never fully embraces Mandela's vision for a rainbow nation, having been too badly hurt by the apartheid regime which deprived her of her father, destroyed her family, and oppressed her people. She is upset by a photograph of Mandela shaking hands with Pienaar, and remains bitter towards the Afrikaner minority. Mandela dismisses this as 'selfish thinking' that 'does not serve the nation' (Scene 11), but audiences cannot help but feel sympathy for Zindzi's position.

Similarly, the Springboks, with the exception of Pienaar, initially resist Mandela's efforts to engage them in the reconciliation process. They cannot see any value in the township coaching clinics, and regard these as an interruption to their training. They refuse to learn the words to 'N'kosi Sikelel' iAfrica', and struggle to see themselves as representative of all South Africans. It is only after the players visit Robben Island and see for themselves how brutally political prisoners were treated under apartheid that they are able to fully appreciate the extent of Mandela's capacity for forgiveness. This excursion brings the team together, and the men are better able to understand the experience of the black population of South Africa. They become more united as a team, and more willing to take their place as a symbol of the whole country. Pienaar reflects this new attitude when he states that they 'had the support of 43 million South Africans' (Scene 26) when they won the World Cup.

Key point

Note that forgiveness and reconciliation are not synonyms. Forgiveness means to stop feeling anger or blame towards someone, while reconciliation involves taking active steps to restore friendly relationships and find ways to make different opinions compatible with each other.

Family and fatherhood

Key quotes

'I have a very large family – 42 million.' (Mandela, Scene 8)

'He's not a saint, OK? He's a man, with a man's problems.' (Linga, Scene 8)

Only two biological families are shown in *Invictus* – that of Francois Pienaar, and a portion of Nelson Mandela's – although the concept of family, particularly fatherhood, is important to the film. Eastwood presents the role of father as largely symbolic, with Mandela identifying himself as father of 'a very large family – 42 million' (Scene 8). This is in stark contrast with the challenging relationship he has with his daughter Zindzi, a relationship that has been irrevocably damaged by his extended incarceration and political activism during Zindzi's youth, as well as by his separation from Winifred Mandela, Zindzi's mother.

Many South Africans regard Mandela as a paternal figure. His age, wisdom and authority reinforce this perception. Jason and Linga greet him in the mornings with a traditional Xhosa greeting that translates as 'I see you, father'. This respectful address demonstrates the high regard the men have for Mandela, as well as endorsing his authority and influence. Black South Africans, in particular, place great faith in Mandela, trusting him to guide them through the difficult post-apartheid years and address the damaging repercussions of decades of white rule. This is especially true of Sipho, who appears to be fatherless and therefore looks to Mandela as a father figure. Mandela responds to this by demonstrating a very paternal style of leadership. His firm but fair approach honours the trust that people place in him, and the best interest of his country is always at the heart of his decisions.

Mandela finds less success in his role as biological father to Zindzi. Their relationship is strained, and Zindzi cancels appointments and is shown to be quite prickly and distant when she is forced to interact with him. Mandela was in prison for much of Zindzi's childhood, a fact she cites with some bitterness when she refers to the police brutality she and her family experienced 'when you were in jail'. This comment is calculated to wound by making Mandela feel guilty, and he responds by accusing her of 'selfish thinking' (Scene 11), a comment that is not well received by Zindzi. The whole exchange illustrates the difficulty Mandela has interacting with his own daughter, highlighting the fact that 'he's a man, with a man's problems' (Scene 8). It is ironic that a man so at ease with strangers finds it so difficult to engage with his own family.

Francois Pienaar's family is more cohesive, although, like Zindzi, Pienaar's political views are quite different from those of his father. While Mr Pienaar is very negative and cynical about the Mandela regime, his son comes to regard Mandela with great warmth and respect. In many ways Francois' values align more closely with Mandela's than with his father's, reinforcing Mandela's role as father to the nation. Mrs Pienaar appears to be more open to change and the prospect of a new South Africa, engaging with Eunice (the Pienaars' maid). However, the family is shown to be quite traditional and conservative, and Mrs Pienaar does not actively go against her husband. It is only when Pienaar includes Eunice in the ticket allocation for the World Cup final that his father seems to become more open to the idea of the rainbow nation.

DIFFERENT INTERPRETATIONS

Different interpretations arise from different responses to a text. Over time, a text will evoke a wide range of responses from its readers, who may come from various social or cultural groups and live in very different places and historical periods. Responses by critics and reviewers can be published in newspapers, journals and books, both online and in print. They can also be expressed in discussions among readers in the media, classrooms, book groups and so on.

While there is no single correct reading or interpretation of a text, it is important to understand that an interpretation is more than a personal opinion – it is the justification of a point of view on the text. To present an interpretation of a text based on your point of view, you must use a logical argument and support it with relevant evidence from the text.

Critical viewpoints

It is generally acknowledged that the story of the Springboks' World Cup victory is an extraordinary one, and most critics respond positively to *Invictus*. It was nominated for many awards, including Oscars and Golden Globes, and received the 2009 National Board of Review Freedom of Expression Award. Many of the awards focused on the way *Invictus* handled the issue of racism in South Africa, with organisations such as the African American Film Critics Association and Black Reel recognising Morgan Freeman with Best Actor trophies.

A quick survey of the critical reception the film received reveals extensive praise of Morgan Freeman, with Bill Keller, in *The Guardian*, describing his performance as 'less an impersonation than an incarnation' (Keller 2010). While some critics noted that Freeman's South African accent occasionally slipped, this is generally seen as a minor flaw in an otherwise excellent performance. Matt Damon, playing Francois Pienaar, attracts similar acclaim. The only criticism of Damon's role in the film seems to be that he was not given enough opportunity to really demonstrate his capabilities.

Some critics who are less than enthusiastic about the film point to Eastwood's sometimes laboured depiction of the rugby matches as a weakness, while others suggest that the film succumbs to what Keller describes as 'the danger of hagiography' in its overly saintly depiction of Mandela (Keller 2010). Ian Buckwalter explains that Eastwood 'hits all the right formula notes of both the inspiring historical biopic and the underdog sports movie, making it impossible to hate. He also hits those notes so insistently ... that he makes it a difficult movie to really love' (Buckwalter 2009). In addition, some critics note that South Africa still has a long way to go before the legacy of apartheid is behind it, contrary to the positive ending of *Invictus* which seems to present the rainbow nation as a fait accompli. It is true that South Africa embraced the Springboks as they campaigned for the 1995 World Cup; however, it is also true that even today there are still very few black players in the Springboks team, and there are still many black South Africans living in extreme poverty. To accept the success implied at the end of *Invictus* seems to require audiences to put aside their knowledge of the ongoing challenges faced by South Africa today.

Two interpretations

Clint Eastwood's *Invictus* is open to a range of interpretations. Many of the different responses arise from the difficulty in definitively classifying the film as a particular genre, which could lead audiences to have a variety of expectations which may or may not be satisfied. Most of the differences of opinion centre on the perceived accuracy of the film, with some audiences applauding Eastwood's adherence to the truth while others reject his version of events. Many of the criticisms centre on the fact that audiences are aware of the limitations of Mandela's success. While few would deny that Mandela's achievements in bringing South Africa close to reconciliation are extraordinary, it is naive to think that a World Cup victory can solve the problems facing this deeply divided nation.

Interpretation 1: *Invictus* presents an inaccurate and romanticised version of reality.

When dealing with a true story, particularly one as well known, and as unlikely, as the story of the 1995 Rugby World Cup final, it is difficult to present a narrative that is both accurate and engaging. The *Australian* newspaper rejects Eastwood's interpretation of events, with an opinion piece taking umbrage at the fact that, in reality, Mandela gave Pienaar a copy of Theodore Roosevelt's 'The Man in the Arena', not 'Invictus' as shown in the film. From this starting point the article goes on to criticise the casting of the Springboks, the filming of the rugby scenes and the omission of the All Black claim that they were poisoned a few days before the game by a waitress called Susie (*The Australian* 2010). Audiences who expect the film to be almost documentary-like in its accuracy are likely to be disappointed by the concessions Eastwood has made to Hollywood expectations.

From the opening scenes of the film, which distil four years into four minutes, the challenges facing Mandela are presented in very broad terms. The dichotomy between black and white South Africa is shown through the juxtaposition of two sports practice grounds, one for the white and privileged, the other for black and impoverished children. References to specific political issues are oblique, with Brenda trying to engage Mandela in politics while he is distracted by the rugby. He is shown to be almost obsessive in his desire to see the Springboks win the World Cup, to the point that he interrupts official meetings and spends his time learning the Springboks' names rather than preparing for a trade summit in Taiwan.

Peter Canavese suggests that '*Invictus* is the sort of movie that, despite hewing fairly closely to the facts, has trouble seeming truthful. Practically everyone behaves like an allegorical symbol rather than a person' (Canavese 2010). Eastwood tries to humanise Mandela by including tense exchanges with his daughter Zindzi, but even this interaction is influenced by the rugby, with Zindzi criticising Mandela for meeting with Pienaar.

Some critics argue that the film oversimplifies the struggles facing Mandela, and South Africa. Alex von Tunzelmann suggests that at the end of the film 'you get the message that world peace has broken out and racism is fixed now' (von Tunzelmann 2013). This is clearly not the case: South Africa and the Springboks still struggle to overcome the aftermath of apartheid. While it is uplifting to watch the country uniting behind the Springboks, security staff learning to work together, and the policemen embracing Sipho, critics reject the implication that the rainbow nation is a reality and that the problems facing South Africa have been resolved by the end of the World Cup final.

Interpretation 2: *Invictus* is an accurate portrayal of the early days of Nelson Mandela's presidency.

Several films and telemovies have been made about the life of Nelson Mandela, and many of these have been criticised for becoming too bogged down in the sheer weight of information available. Bill Keller notes that despite attempts to write a screenplay for *Long Walk to Freedom*, 'Mandela's sprawling memoir proved too unwieldy for a film' (Keller 2010), and it was not until Carlin (author of the biography that inspired *Invictus*) identified 'an event that distils the essence of Mandela's genius, and the essence of the South African miracle' (Carlin 2010) that the film really gained traction. Some critics argue that by focusing on one aspect of Mandela's presidency it is possible to summarise the early years, making it easier to convey the impact he had on his nation.

While it is true that Mandela is shown to be almost obsessive in his pursuit of the World Cup victory, audiences are frequently reminded that this is 'a political calculation' (Scene 7). By focusing the audiences' attention on various sub-groups of South African society Eastwood illustrates the impact Mandela's endorsement of the Springboks has on all South Africans. The developing relationship between the ANC and Special Branch security teams, brought together by a combination of their respect for Mandela and a growing mutual understanding of rugby, is representative of the improving relations between black and white South

Africans across the country. This is further illustrated by the increasingly relaxed interactions between Sipho and the Afrikaner policemen outside Ellis Park Stadium. Similarly, the increasing confidence of Pienaar and his team mirrors the gradual acceptance by the Afrikaners of Mandela's leadership.

Rugby is a focus of the film only insofar as it provides a vehicle that allows Eastwood to present the growing unity within South Africa. Eastwood, like Mandela, uses the Springboks as a symbol to bring the nation together. In *Invictus*, Mandela's purpose never waivers – everything he does is designed to create a 'rainbow nation', and in order to achieve this he must temper his 'political calculation' with an equally important 'human calculation' (Scene 7). While Eastwood has indeed used some symbols and stereotypes to convey meaning, he has remained true to the spirit of the period and has accurately represented the challenges of Mandela's early days as president as well as the joy, the national pride and the exuberance of the World Cup victory. When Pienaar tells Nerine that 'tomorrow's taken care of, one way or another' (Scene 19) he is not just referring to the World Cup final. He is acknowledging that South Africa still has a long journey ahead before it is truly the 'rainbow nation', but he also recognises that Mandela has set a clear direction for his people.

QUESTIONS & ANSWERS

This section focuses on your own analytical writing on the text, and gives you strategies for producing high-quality responses in your coursework and exam essays.

Essay writing – an overview

An essay on a literary work is a formal and serious piece of writing that presents your point of view on the text, usually in response to a given topic. Your 'point of view' in an essay is your interpretation of the meaning of the text's language, structure, characters, situations and events, supported by detailed analysis of textual evidence.

Analyse – don't summarise

In your essays it is important to avoid simply summarising what happens in a text.

- A **summary** is a description or paraphrase (retelling in different words) of the characters and events. For example: 'Macbeth has a horrifying vision of a dagger dripping with blood before he goes to murder King Duncan.'
- An **analysis** is an explanation of the real meaning or significance that lies 'beneath' the text's words (and images, for a film). For example: 'Macbeth's vision of a bloody dagger shows how deeply uneasy he is about the violent act he is contemplating, and conveys his sense that supernatural forces are impelling him to act.'

A limited amount of summary is sometimes necessary to let your reader know which part of the text you wish to discuss. However, always keep this to a minimum and follow it immediately with your analysis of what this part of the text is really telling us.

Plan your essay

Carefully plan your essay so that you have a clear idea of what you are going to say. The plan ensures that your ideas flow logically, that your argument remains consistent and that you stay on the topic. An essay plan should be a list of **brief dot points** covering no more than half a page.

- Include your central argument or main contention – a concise statement of your overall response to the topic.
- Write three or four dot points for each paragraph, indicating the main idea and evidence/examples from the text. Note that in your essay you will need to *expand* on these points and *analyse* the evidence.

Structure your essay

An essay is a complete, self-contained piece of writing. It has a clear beginning (the introduction), middle (several body paragraphs) and end (the last paragraph or conclusion). It must also have a central argument that runs throughout, linking each paragraph to form a coherent whole. See examples of introductions and conclusions in the 'Analysing a sample topic' and 'Sample answer' sections.

The introduction establishes your overall response to the topic. It includes your main contention and outlines the main evidence you will refer to in the course of the essay. Write your introduction *after* you have done a plan and *before* you write the rest of the essay.

The body paragraphs argue your case – they present evidence from the text and explain how this evidence supports your argument. Each body paragraph needs:

- a strong **topic sentence** (usually the first sentence) that states the main point being made in the paragraph
- **evidence** from the text, including some brief quotations
- **analysis** of the textual evidence, with **explanation** of its significance and how it supports your argument
- **links back to the topic** in one or more statements, usually towards the end of the paragraph.

Connect the body paragraphs so that your discussion flows smoothly. Use some linking words and phrases such as 'similarly' and 'on the other hand', though don't start every paragraph like this. Another strategy is to use a significant word from the last sentence of one paragraph in the first sentence of the next.

Use key terms from the topic – or synonyms for them – throughout, so the relevance of your discussion to the topic is always clear.

The conclusion ties everything together and finishes the essay. It includes strong statements that emphasise your central argument and provide a clear response to the topic.

Avoid simply restating the points made earlier in the essay – this will end on a very flat note and imply that you have run out of ideas and vocabulary. The conclusion should be a logical extension of what you have written, not just a repetition or summary of it. Writing an effective conclusion can be a challenge. Try using these tips:

- Start by linking back to the final sentence of the second-last paragraph – this helps your writing to flow, rather than leaping back to your main contention straight away.
- Use synonyms and expressions with equivalent meanings to vary your vocabulary. This allows you to reinforce your line of argument without being repetitive.
- When planning your essay, think of one or two broad statements or observations about the text's wider meaning. These should be related to the topic and your overall argument. Keep them for the conclusion, since they will give you something 'new' to say but still follow logically from your discussion. The introduction will be focused on the topic, but the conclusion can present a wider view of the text.

Essay topics

1 'Both Mandela and Pienaar use words as their most powerful tools.' Discuss.

2 'Eastwood suggests that, to win over the nation, Mandela must first win over the media.'
Do you agree?

3 How does *Invictus* show that forgiveness is more effective than revenge?

4 'Mandela's most important achievement is that he provides hope.' Do you agree?

5 "If Madiba can do it, we can do it."
'*Invictus* demonstrates that the most effective leaders lead by example.' Discuss.

6 "Tomorrow's taken care of, one way or another."
To what extent does *Invictus* suggest that people must address the past in order to create a future?

7 'Eastwood's use of cinematic techniques enhances the narrative in *Invictus*.' Discuss.

8 How are language and symbols used in *Invictus* to unite or divide the nation?

9 "Times change, and we need to change as well."
'*Invictus* suggests that reconciliation is dependent on all people having the capacity to change.' Do you agree?

10 How does *Invictus* explore the idea of fatherhood?

Vocabulary for writing on *Invictus*

Afrikaans: a language of southern Africa, derived from Dutch. It is spoken mostly by white Afrikaner South Africans.

Afrikaner: an Afrikaans-speaking white South African, particularly one descended from the Dutch settlers.

Apartheid: a legal framework that separated black, white and coloured South Africans from each other. It was dismantled in 1991.

Boer: a member of the Dutch and Huguenot population which settled in southern Africa in the late seventeenth century. The Boers' present-day descendants are the Afrikaners.

Cut: in film, a break between two shots.

Mise en scène: the arrangement of scenery, props and people within a frame in a film.

Montage: a series of short shots edited together, often accompanied by music or a voice-over, designed to show time passing.

Scene: a particular segment of a film that shows action in a single location over a continuous time. This is different from the 'Scenes' or chapters identified on a DVD for navigation purposes, which will typically include several scenes.

Shot: a continuous section of film that is not interrupted by a cut.

Township: an underdeveloped and impoverished area inhabited by the black and coloured people of South Africa. Townships were established to minimise interactions between black and white South Africans.

Xhosa: the second-largest ethnic group in South Africa, and the name of its language. Mandela is Xhosa.

Analysing a sample topic

"If Madiba can do it, we can do it."

'*Invictus* demonstrates that the most effective leaders lead by example.' Discuss.

This topic invites you to consider the various types of leadership shown within the film, and to assess the effectiveness of each. While it might be tempting to focus your attention solely on the leadership styles of Mandela and Pienaar, try to ensure you always include some acknowledgement of secondary characters in your response. This reveals a more considered and detailed interpretation of the text.

Your first step when planning an essay is to ensure you understand the key elements of the topic. In this case, you need to have a clear interpretation of the key words – 'most effective leaders', 'by example' – as well as the origin of the quote provided: Jason makes this statement when he is speaking to the white security guards about Mandela's busy schedule. Finally, you must also be aware of the instruction, which is 'discuss', in this instance. Once you are sure you understand these aspects of the topic, you can brainstorm ideas, drawing on your knowledge of the text's themes, characters and construction.

When addressing this topic you could consider the obvious leadership shown by Mandela and Pienaar, but also the developing leadership skills of Jason Tshabalala. While the quote directs you towards leading by example, you could also argue that the most effective leadership requires more – it also involves teaching others to lead, as well as providing inspiration. This is demonstrated most clearly by Mandela as he prepares Pienaar and Jason to lead others. While this topic does not ask you to focus specifically on film techniques, it is important to support your discussion with evidence that includes some reference to the cinematic strategies used by Eastwood.

Sample introduction

> Through the character of Nelson Mandela, Clint Eastwood's film *Invictus* demonstrates that the most effective strategy for leadership is to lead by example, and to inspire others to follow. When Jason Tshabalala says, 'If Madiba can do it, we can', he is holding Mandela up as an inspiration. Francois Pienaar takes a similar approach in his position as captain of the Springboks, ensuring he is always the first to take on a challenge. Both Pienaar and Jason benefit from Mandela's guidance and develop their own authority as a result, suggesting that the most effective leaders provide inspiration, even when that example may not be the most popular course of action.

Body paragraph outline

Paragraph 1: Effective leaders lead by example.

- When Mandela walks into the Union Buildings on his first day as president he advises the largely Afrikaner staff that 'what's past is past', and assures them that he will not disqualify anyone on the basis of their language or skin colour. In this way he models forgiveness, and thus inspires others to be equally forgiving.
- Mandela wears a Springbok rugby jersey to the World Cup final, providing a highly visible symbol of his support of the team and thus encouraging all South Africans, regardless of colour, to join him in supporting the Springboks. In this scene Eastwood emphasises unity through the prominent placement of the new South African flag and also through the use of background music.
- When Pienaar asks anything of his team, he makes it clear he is willing to do the same himself. When training he is the first to throw himself into drills; when visiting the townships he is the first to support Mandela's request. By modelling the behaviour he expects, Pienaar is able to inspire his team to follow.

Paragraph 2: Effective leaders prepare others for leadership.

- Mandela supports Pienaar in developing his already strong leadership skills. Through conversation and affirmation, Mandela demonstrates the power of inclusive language, a strategy which Pienaar uses in the final moments of the World Cup final to motivate his team. Eastwood emphasises this through mise en scène when Pienaar is having afternoon tea with Mandela. While the men are initially shown in separate shots, as they begin to discuss their shared understanding of leadership the two men are shown in the same shot, illustrating their growing connection.
- Mandela also guides Jason towards tolerance and effective leadership. When Jason first meets the Afrikaner security team he tells Mandela they cannot work together; however, by the time the World Cup final is played he is leading a diverse security team. Jason is inspired by Mandela's capacity for forgiveness, and in time Jason is able to work comfortably with the Afrikaners. Eastwood demonstrates this growing relationship by positioning the Afrikaner and black characters progressively physically closer together, culminating in an informal rugby match between them.
- Pienaar not only leads his team by example, he also allows other team members an opportunity to shine. This is particularly clear in the case of Chester, who is encouraged to take the lead during the township coaching clinics and again when he is asked to guide the team in a final prayer after its World Cup victory. The increasing level of teamwork is shown throughout the film as the Springboks begin to move together in a progressively more synchronised way during their training runs.

Paragraph 3: Leading by example, and with good intentions, makes it possible to achieve things that could not be done otherwise.

- Mandela's support is derived largely from the fact that the people know he will not ask them to do anything he is not willing to do himself. As a result, even if his decisions are unpalatable, people are still likely to support him. This is seen when he asks the National Sports Council to 'let me lead you now' in voting to retain the Springbok name and colours. He knows that his request will be met with opposition, but relies on his political capital and the trust the people have in his judgement – a trust built up through the example he sets.

- Pienaar draws on a similar foundation for support. When he asks the team to learn the words to 'N'kosi Sikelel' iAfrika', he is willing to do this himself. He accepts Mandela's challenge to lead the Springboks to victory in the World Cup, and finds ways to inspire the team through music, words and his own example.
- This is in contrast with less effective leaders, such as members of the National Sports Council. Their decision to abolish the Springbok name, emblem and colours comes from a place of fear and revenge. Mandela is able to sway them by providing a more positive vision, allowing for the possibility of reconciliation rather than a continuation of hostility.

Sample conclusion

Mandela's ability to lead by example is what ultimately allows him to achieve success. His willingness to forgive the apartheid regime is instrumental in showing other South Africans that the cycle of fear and hatred can be broken. He models the attitudes he hopes to inspire in others and, as a result, the people around him are willing to follow his guidance. Pienaar uses Mandela's strategies to guide the Springboks to victory, and Jason is inspired by Mandela's capacity for forgiveness and learns to work with the Afrikaner security team. Eastwood suggests that the most effective leaders not only lead by example, they also inspire others to greatness and have an ultimate goal that is seen to be positive.

SAMPLE ANSWER

'Both Mandela and Pienaar use words as their most powerful tools.' Discuss.

While Mandela and Pienaar both rely on words as a means of influencing others, Clint Eastwood's *Invictus* suggests that, in fact, their actions have the greatest impact. Mandela's ability to speak a range of languages allows him to communicate directly with a range of people, inspiring trust and connection. In contrast, Pienaar only communicates in Afrikaans or English, which limits his verbal interactions. However, both men are able to positively influence those around them through a combination of their own words, their actions, and their considered use of the words of others. While words can be used to divide, Mandela and Pienaar both demonstrate that words are powerful weapons against the racism, fear, and other issues confronting post-apartheid South Africa, particularly when supported by actions that create an atmosphere in which the words can be truly heard.

South Africa in the late twentieth century is a nation divided along ethnic lines, with each group having its own distinct language and culture. This makes it very difficult for the disparate groups to communicate, exacerbating the division between them. The multilingual Nelson Mandela is able to bridge the gap because he is able to make genuine connections with people, using inclusive language and addressing them in their own tongue. Mandela recognises this when he speaks (in Xhosa) to the National Sports Council, saying he learned Afrikaans while in prison so he could 'prevail against' the Afrikaner regime. This linguistic knowledge is invaluable from the earliest moments of Mandela's presidency, when he placates his Afrikaner staff by addressing them in Afrikaans. Just as Mandela cannot relate to his staff if he is 'hiding behind men with guns', he also prefers not to hide behind a translator. It is his actions – in learning the Afrikaner language and culture, and engaging directly with people – that are truly effective. Without Mandela's warm engagement and positive role-modelling, it seems unlikely he would achieve the same degree of success, regardless of his carefully chosen words.

In contrast to Mandela, Francois Pienaar is only shown interacting verbally with those who speak Afrikaans or English. Despite this he is an effective leader, inspiring his team to be 'better than they think they can be' and leading them to victory in the World Cup. He uses words to unite the team, borrowing Mandela's strategy of using inclusive language to cement them together with a common goal. He also draws on the words of others to reinforce his position, particularly 'N'kosi Sikelel' iAfrica', the new South African anthem, which he uses to encourage unity within the team as well as among the spectators. In addition, and perhaps more powerfully, Pienaar inspires his team by leading by example. He is the first to jump up and run when the coach seems to be pushing the team beyond exhaustion; he is vocal in support of Mandela's approach, even when this meets with resistance from some team members; and he embraces the role of the Springboks as 'more than just a rugby team'.

Pienaar's leadership does not stop with his team. He also provides a public face for Mandela's 'rainbow nation', providing a focus for the support of '43 million' South Africans. By embracing Mandela's challenge to 'win the World Cup', Pienaar demonstrates to his team and his country that he accepts the new regime and will work with Mandela to achieve unity. His words are powerful in leading his team, but without the actions to support them his words would be less influential.

One of the most important ideas in *Invictus* is the power of words to influence others, whether positively or negatively. This power is derived as much from the intention of the speaker as it is from the words themselves, suggesting that words do not function independently of actions. When Mandela's Afrikaner and black security teams first work together, Etienne and the other Afrikaner staff speak together in Afrikaans, deliberately excluding Jason and his team. The words themselves are fairly innocuous, being a comment on Mandela's busy schedule; however, their power to divide the two security teams is undeniable.

Jason retaliates by referring to Mandela as 'Madiba', his clan name, and Etienne's assertion that they will 'call him Mr President' further cements the differences between the two groups. These different terms of address for Mandela do not change throughout the film, but as the security team becomes more unified the words simply represent difference rather than division. For both Jason and Etienne, the specific words they use are of secondary importance to the meaning invested in them by the speaker.

Invictus demonstrates that words are a powerful tool, but their true power derives from the purpose and actions of the speaker. It does not matter how eloquently Mandela pleads for unity if he does not himself model the forgiveness and acceptance required to achieve reconciliation. Similarly, Pienaar is able to inspire his team through words only when the words are accompanied by positive actions. Even those who use words to divide, such as Jason and Etienne, come to realise that this division actually arises from their intentions rather than the words themselves. Eastwood's *Invictus* demonstrates that while words are powerful tools that can manipulate, guide and inspire, without actions and purpose to support them this power is greatly diminished.

REFERENCES AND READING

Text

Invictus 2009, dir. Clint Eastwood, Warner Bros. Pictures. Starring Morgan Freeman and Matt Damon.

Online resources

Buckwalter, Ian 2009, 'Out of frame: Invictus', *DCist*, 11 December, http://dcist.com/2009/12/invictus.php

Canavese, Peter 2010, 'Invictus', *Groucho Reviews*, 30 May, http://www.grouchoreviews.com/reviews/3655

History.com 2010, 'Apartheid', http://www.history.com/topics/apartheid

Keller, Bill 2010, 'Morgan Freeman's long walk to Nelson Mandela', *The Guardian*, 1 January, https://www.theguardian.com/film/2009/dec/31/morgan-freeman-nelson-mandela-invictus

Mandela, Nelson 1964, Trial Speech transcript, https://www.nelsonmandela.org/news/entry/i-am-prepared-to-die

Mitchell, Brittany 2015, '1995 World Cup: unifying a divided nation', *ESPN*, 23 June, http://en.espn.co.uk/southafrica/rugby/story/267173.html

Nauright, John 2013, 'Mandela saw sport as a way to bring South Africans together', *The Conversation*, 7 December, http://theconversation.com/mandela-saw-sport-as-a-way-to-bring-south-africans-together-21244

The 16th Man 2010, dir. Clifford Bestall, ESPN Films. Narrated by Morgan Freeman. https://www.youtube.com/watch?v=U2htysgr6-Y

The Australian 2010, 'Invictus not averse to playing with facts', 25 January, http://www.theaustralian.com.au/sport/opinion/invictus-not-averse-to-playing-with-facts/news-story/f356b2a3a6f7c92454752304c5d02434?sv=fb45e974496ad52f945d968f1e65d90a von Tunzelmann, Alex 2013, 'Invictus: better on Nelson Mandela than rugby', *The Guardian*, 3 October, https://www.theguardian.com/film/filmblog/2013/oct/03/invictus-nelson-mandela-rugby-clint-eastwood-reel-history

Further reading

Carlin, John 2010, *Invictus: Nelson Mandela and the Game that Made a Nation*, Penguin Books, New York.

Henley, William Ernest 1888, 'Invictus', http://poemhunter.com/poem/invictus/

Mandela, Nelson 1994, *Long Walk to Freedom*, Little, Brown and Company, New York.